THE CHANGING VATICAN

THE
CHANGING
VATICAN

ALBERTO CAVALLARI

TRANSLATED BY
RAYMOND T. KELLY

DOUBLEDAY & COMPANY, INC.
GARDEN CITY, NEW YORK
1967

IL VATICANO CHE CAMBIA, by Alberto Cavallari
published in Italy
by Arnoldo Mondadori Editore
© Arnoldo Mondadori Editore, 1966

CONTENTS

5

PREFACE

The purpose of this book is to present to the reader, in a considerably expanded way, a series of articles and reports written for Milan's *Corriere della Sera* between October and December, 1965. It includes, of course, the talk I had with Pope Paul VI, which has been called the first papal interview in history; but I have expressly avoided any reference in the title to that interview so as not to give the book a tone of sensationalism, to which it does not aspire. THE CHANGING VATICAN, like my other books, is a work of journalism; it makes no claim to expertise in Vatican affairs, nor does it pretend to the depth of a specialist's report. Its sole aim is to bear witness to one of the great issues of our time: the renewal of the Catholic Church.

The reader, Catholic or otherwise, will not find in these pages an analysis of the Church of Rome as "an organization of believers" or as "a mystical body." What is described is that Church as a historical institution, and my point of view is always journalistic and always limited to institutional, political, and sociological aspects. Thus, while the book may contribute to an understanding of the Vatican and its structure, it is not a theological work, nor a chronicle of events, nor a study in depth of the Vatican either as a state or as the Holy See.

I have refrained from naming those persons whose kindness and cooperation have enabled me to write this book because, the subject being what it is, such acknowledgment might appear to be name-dropping or, worse still, an attempt to preclude criticism of any errors, for which I alone am responsible. Such persons, nonetheless, are aware of my gratitude.

A. C.

INTRODUCTION

Inside the Vatican

At the end of 1965, the Second Vatican Council was closing and the Vatican was going through a phase that many nations experience as they terminate a "constitutional convention." Delusions and hopes intermingle; signs of renewal are accompanied by signs of weakness; the constitution represents at best only a nebulous vision of the future for a society that sets out to travel new paths. What I proposed to do at that time was to examine that analogous situation, that period of uncertainty and growth for the Vatican, so as to understand how the Vatican changes, if it does change, to determine how deep certain changes are, and to register all this in direct and simple terms with no particular concern for the structure of the finished product.

My reason for feeling the need for such a work is obvious. Millions of persons are watching the Vatican of the sixties. No civil or religious capital in the world, whether Washington, Moscow, or Calcutta, is under the spotlight to the extent that the Vatican is, for no capital is living such years of obvious transition. But to grasp what is happening is not easy when one takes an outside position, whether that position be sympathetic or otherwise, or when one confuses change in externals with change in

8

substance, or, when one pays sole attention to the abstract ideas involved. What is needed is to see the Vatican "from the inside," to obtain the optical reverse of what we see "from the outside." We need to fix directly not on the ideas generated or on the waves caused by the impulses which were given, but on the voices of the protagonists, on the variability of a process already under way, on the apparently arbitrary nature of its flow. The full meaning of these events in the Catholic Church does not yet lend itself to a complete rationalization, and thus the observer also has to deal with the problem of the techniques best suited to describing these realities. It seemed to me that only the age-old formula of the diary, so useful for an uninhibited recording of one's impressions, so elastic in language, so ready to correct itself and to indicate its essential limitations at any point, was quite appropriate for reflecting such a dynamic process.

It is not only Catholics whose eyes are following this dramatic period in Vatican history. Adherents to different confessions definitely consider themselves involved in the operation of religious pacification, or ecumenism, initiated by Rome. The Communist countries cannot ignore Rome's "dialogue" with atheism, which invites them to the forum. Certain Vatican political positions which matured during the years of the "constitutional convention" and which incline toward overcoming the preponderance of the world blocs, coincide with the interests of the weak or neutral countries and make the events of Rome daily more interesting, even in purely political terms, in Afro-Asian eyes. There is the exception of Red China, which officially ignores but is not ignored by, the Vatican. The visit of Paul VI to the United Nations and his messages to Mao Tse-tung have not modified the situation, but it is a question of an understandable retaliation; Peking omits from its world map those parts of the West that have not yet put the new China on their own maps.

It is inevitable that we ask what makes up a Vatican that is able to display so many appealing sides. To be sure, we will never have completely satisfying answers to the question. We have at best only sketches, vague suggestions, a description of such features as are taking shape. Continuity remains a basic characteristic of Catholic power and of all its structures. But there are historical phases in which this continuity, like the earth revolving in space, projects varying shadows around itself. At the present moment, Roman continuity is tracing another of its parabolas. And we need more elastic instruments than usual in order to register it.

The Vatican of today is definitely something mobile and flowing. This concept is just beginning to be taken into account, and it calls for continuous adjustments in our conception of the Vatican. The transition from the years of Pius XII to these of Paul VI has put in motion, after the Johannine reshuffling of things, a complex of forces that insinuate themselves continuously—even when they seem exhausted, contradicted, or crystallized. But such an interplay of forces and counterforces can be detected only when observed from within. And only when the seismograph that registers them reflects also their elasticity will their true significance be revealed.

Paul VI is himself a proof of how risky it is to judge things "from the outside." Those same voices which in 1964 stigmatized him as a suffocator of the Council are now exalting him as the intrepid defender of religious liberty—which is of course equally a caricature. Hence to see as much as possible "from the inside" was my constant concern. I took equal care, however, to maintain my perspective as a layman. I had no intention of discussing religious questions, of siding with the progressive or the conservative elements in the Church, or of judging any decisions to be beneficial or harmful for the future of Catholics. I thought it would be useful to describe the Vatican transformations in relation to the Church immersed in the "conciliar shift"; to see what new organisms were born and how the old organisms in the shadow of St. Peter's are being transformed; and then to register what certain theological and philosophical *aggiornamenti* mean for an international institution such as the Holy See. I have taken as a firm rule that this account should have a flexibility corresponding to that of the reality I observed, and I have generally preferred explanations to judgments, questions to answers, statements to criticisms. I have striven to see how a certain complex historical situation is being lived by the different men directly involved in it, whatever my own judgment may be.

For an Italian journalist to carry out a mission in the Vatican is to make the shortest of possible voyages. In the morning, he has only to cross the Tiber to reach the little state. In the evening, he has only to recross it to return to Italy. The trip thus becomes a daily routine which probably diminishes the detachment we tend to presume in a traveler, and which may provoke, in the reader himself, a sense of Vaticanism and officialdom. There is, in fact, a common conviction that one cannot see the Vatican "from within" without being an "insider" in the Vatican—that is, without being tied by secret connections to a world that has made a myth of the secret, without being linked to it by relationships of confidence and support, or at least by a mutual protective and opportunistic understanding. But the very existence of this account perhaps proves that something else is possible. I do not want to say that "secretness" no longer exists, simply because a layman like myself, representing a lay newspaper, was able to have such an uninhibited experience. Many, Catholics included, regarded my mission in the Vatican as suspect and as "privileged," even as "instrumentalized."[1] But the fact remains that such a mission was permitted. Without inducing a fixed rule from a personal case, we can nonetheless conclude that it does reflect something new. Perhaps this also forms a part of the changes of the conciliar period, and is an aspect of the new Vatican image which calls for continuous readjustment and continuous rethinking on the part of observers who, like myself, try to begin from zero with direct experience of a world so subject to discussion.

To conceive of the Vatican by beginning at the beginning (putting aside the significance for Italy of the papal domination, of the Church-state polemic, and of a controversial pontificate like that of Pius XII) certainly requires a special effort for Italians. But then it is not easy for any European to have a true vision of the Vatican, in view of the present cultural struggles, of our progressive inclinations, and of the ascendant technocratic philosophies. For it is a fact that we tend to regard ideologies today as incomplete, as capable of modification and transformation, and in fact as on the wane in a world destined to the triumphs of a practical technology which levels everything and everybody. At the same time, there is a Catholic resistance to having the Vatican known as it really is. Many in the Vatican live in fact as proponents of the Church's "eternal" and "immutable" image, as protagonists of a worldly sagacity based upon the "secret" and upon other techniques of behavior.[2] (These techniques sometimes produce amusing results. For example, every summer the news spreads that Paul VI is threatened by an obscure malady. I was told that this happens because Cardinal Tisserant goes to Castelgandolfo to extend to the pope his wishes for a good vacation, and he delivers a talk—always the same—to the pilgrims collected there, on the pope being fatigued by overwork and on his collaborators being concerned for his health. This laudative talk always ends up engendering suspicion, for it seems to be alluding to, but covering up, some reality. But no one confirms it, and no one denies it; and so the newspapers announce that Paul VI is gravely ill.) There is even a certain snobbism connected with Vatican secrecy, which gives rise to the art of Vaticanology. It could be regarded as a sort of apotheosis of clericalism, a kind of arch-clerical defense in the face of an anticlerical polemic, and it becomes a continuous flight from anyone seeking objective knowledge.

Apart from all this, there are many things which justify approaching the Vatican with understanding. If it is true that, with the Second Vatican Council, Catholicism tends to begin again from zero—i.e., bringing the Church of the Inquisition to the point of preaching respect for atheists and religious liberty—it is only just that the observer should also try to start with a clean slate. Rather than try to explain what the Vatican is, I have therefore preferred the effort of learning to understand it. In this sense, the book is only an experimental work. It is experimental in the immediacy of the errors of which I may be guilty, in the fortuitousness of the encounters it relates, in the liberty of my observations, in the laymanlike impropriety of my language, and also in its being an attempt to keep a chronicle while many are crying down the fissure between two cultures.[3]

In the minds of many, the Vatican projects a picture-book image: a too perfect print of pilgrims, nuns, priests, monsignori, Berninis, Swiss guards, fountains, carriages, carriage men, ash trays in show windows, Paul VI on postcards, the sun through the colonnades, the obelisk, *questurini*, clouds, council fathers in violet against a background of rose-gray stone. We usually think that to live "inside" entails a complicated voyage in the world of traditional Vaticanism and the pontifical directory, with perspectives à la Chirico, of the red and yellow mannequins of the papal guard, the corporal dozing next to his halberd, the coming and going through mysterious staircases, the good mornings to the blue and silver papal footman, to the monsignori, to an Excellency, to an Eminence, to the minute-taker, the consultant, the officer of the day, the qualifier, the cup servant, the archivist, the chamber notary, the attaché, the staff master, the head usher, the chief supernumerary, the sacristan, the court herald, the stable-master, the bearer of the golden rose, the court chaplain, the court preacher, and the bookkeeper.[4] We imagine a world of ceremonious courtesy existing within colored loggias, with windows overlooking Rome, inside a Chinese box of offices, salons, drawing rooms, and passages. We conjure up whispered and mysterious conversations in the evening darkness, when soft lights are lit and the Swiss mannequins don their most metaphysical dark gray uniform, while beyond the windows Rome is a blaze of lights surrounding an island in semidarkness called the Vatican.

None of this will be found in the account I have kept. And it is not an omission aimed at demonstrating the nonexistence of such a Vatican. The choreographic and courtier's Vatican, and the "sanctuary" Vatican, do exist; and the faithful chronicle cannot pass them over in silence. But it is lacking in my pages because these Vaticans burst forth for the most part only on days of great celebration, or are revealed to people whose experience is different from mine. For me, to "travel" the Vatican did not mean an encounter with a folklore state or an ancient palace full of intrigues, but an encounter with the Holy See—which means with an ideological capital laden with new and changed problems. As a matter of fact, it is only by habit that I call it "Vatican," this capital which is better and more correctly described as the Holy See. And it is definitely a sign of the times that the Vatican strikes the observer like a Washington or a Moscow without territory, inhabited by a ruling class surprisingly free of clerical complications. Such a Vatican eclipses the colors, the backgrounds, and the typical figures of its classical image. What I saw was Vatican 1965, a capital in the midst of an exceptional year, while the conciliar interval was closing and the post-conciliar period was beginning. I was moving in a world that was less and less an eighteenth-century print, and more and more alive and attentive to new world perspectives and to the great ideological questions of our day. Perhaps as a result my diary turns out to be rather gray, colorless in the attempt to be neutral, incapable of conveying the old images while at the same time unable to propose new ones. But the period I am describing is that of a *turning point* for the Catholic Church, and what I had to do was to explain it to myself before trying to explain it to my readers. Every morning, I went up the Via della Conciliazione, after the bend of the Tiber, conscious of being and determined to remain basically an outside observer. But every morning, I tried to pick up, exclusively from the inside, the images of this turning point. I began in February. Then came spring, summer, and fall. There even arrived the day when my researches penetrated into the least accessible and deepest "inside" of the Vatican. The first pages of my diary were, in fact, to register an unusual conversation.

CHAPTER I

Three Flashbacks on the Council

I recall particularly three things about Vatican II. The first took place on a misty fall morning in 1965, and it gave me an opportunity to step aside from all my unfinished work and to look at it all from another angle. It was the rare opportunity, for a layman, of entering St. Peter's and of sitting among the bishops, of seeing how ideas destined to renew Catholic positions are born and given tangible shape. I found myself in the long line of cars that carried 2500 bishops and cardinals every day along the Tiber. I had the sensation, in the cloud of exhaust fumes, of being a stand-in in the council spectacle. Catholic rhetoric (to which I too contributed in my newspaper articles) has already described these daily scenes: Rome; Hadrian's Tomb; finding oneself immersed in the "river of Catholicism"; a square dotted with myriads of red men; the sensation of participating in a fluid force; a pluralistic and diversified force advancing, in spite of all adversity, with constant aims and in a direction of which it is clearly aware. But to speak in terms of only a spectacle is to miss the reality. It would be more precise to say that the atmosphere was like a convocation of general states. First the black sedans of the cardinals rolled by. Then, more numerous, chartered buses loaded with red birettas, and little Fiats with two or three bishops squeezed in. Negroes in purple robes but with tin crosses got off the city buses. Dutch bishops with wooden crosses limped along on foot. What really struck one was the wave that overran the little Vatican every morning for three years, stealing the show from the papal bureaucracy, breaking the enchantment of Roman folklore, and transforming the myth of the "smallest state in the center of the largest kingdom in the world."

To be sure, yesterday's distinctions still stand. There is the Vatican as a state, with its 110 acres of land and its thousand inhabitants. There is the Vatican as the Holy See, or as the head of the Catholic institution. There is the Vatican as the center of the Church—the mystical body, an "idea evidenced by its believers" rather than an institution.[1] It would help immensely to determine which of these Vaticans was subject to the influence of the council, but it is not easy to make headway through such subtle distinctions. Undoubtedly, all three—the state, the institution, and the idea—were touched upon by the "convocation of the States General" in various ways. Whatever else it did, the council came to grips with all of them. Two thousand five hundred men, recruited from everywhere—Asia, Africa, Europe, and America—a most democratic recruitment (rooted in every social class and nation of the world), and selected in the most aristocratic method possible (they had been consecrated bishops and cardinals through the authority of the pope), formed here an international, a supernational, a super-continental assembly. Although the use of such words as "democratic" and "aristocratic" may be subject to criticism, that is how the council elite strikes an observer. Here was the ruling class which, for three years, subjected the Vatican to the impact of its various theses and attitudes. And the changing Vatican reflects this mobile aristocracy that changes while remaining basically the same, this dynamic aristocracy that disputes, discusses, breaks up into groups, finds its own unity and its own logic daily, but always leaves the traces of a violent passage.

In St. Peter's, where the work is under way, the light of day filters through the windows and mingles with the light of the great chandeliers over the heads of the bishops. The bishops are seated on the red benches that rise like stairs in the grandstands running the length of the nave. We are reminded of Titian's "Council of Trent" with its few seats and its altar, so different from today's assembly, which has about it the ancient force of congresses and major parliaments.[2] The rest of the basilica, surrounding the grandstands with the tombs of popes, statues of saints, marble sculptures, and gold, is in semidarkness. The scene that greets one is lit by tempered light, as in paintings where colors are "internal," producing their own light from within.

Bishops by the hundreds fill the main grandstands right and left. The cardinals, in rows of ten, sit in a section reserved for them at the end of the left grandstand. At the end, across the center platform and closing the rectangle of graded seats, are the tables of the presidents and moderators. In the same area, two small sectors, not filled with red and violet, catch one's eye. One is occupied by Catholic observers: laymen, sisters who head religious orders, and laywomen who are leaders in Catholic organizations. The other sector is more interesting: here sit the observers of the "separated churches"; Protestants in black suits, Waldenses, Russian priests with Rasputin-length hair. This is the section of the "schismatics" and "heretics," located only a step from the altar raised over the tomb of St. Peter. Needless to say, this is the "historical" corner. Ecumenism takes on concrete form here, and is translated into faces, beards, schisms, and heresies that have returned for the first time into the temple of temples of Catholicism. From a purely visual point of view, one has here a tangible experience of the attempt at conciliation being lived in these years. Apart from its ideological implications, one has the physical sensation of the "dialogues" and "openings." Protestants and Orthodox take notes, discuss, are truly involved. Laymen and observers, as myself, are left alone, free to mix among the bishops and even to hear the most heated debates.

During my presence there, for example, the things discussed were delicate, to say the least. Clashes and oral duels on the new problems of the Christian family, on birth control, etc., were everyday occurrences, and the storm was brewing. Cardinal Ruffini is scheduled to speak. It is commonly known that the "progressive" Cardinals Suenens and Léger would give him a fight. The battle will take place here on the floor. It will not be a "filtered down," formal debate, but the real thing. One can circulate freely, enter into the grandstands, listen from the midst of the bishops and follow their reactions inches away. From the top of a grandstand, the only layman in a suit among hundreds of red mantles, I can see how such encounters take place and appreciate the logic that permeates them. If anyone says that debate was lacking in the council, he is wrong. To be sure, no orator responded to the other directly. But the interweaving of the interventions made possible even open clashes of opinions. And that is what I experienced so tangibly in the meeting of the council that took place before my eyes on that unforgettable morning when the conflict between the "progressives" and the "conservatives" became a duel, a pitched battle, a genuine debate in every sense of the word.

The duel begins. Cardinal Ruffini, who is seated at the presidential table, rises to speak. The secretary general of the council makes the announcement from the microphone, and there is a scurrying of bishops to their places after the walks they take from time to time about the basilica floor. Ruffini then speaks into the silence; his voice rises, animated and stirring, and his Latin address develops into a Ciceronian oration. The Cardinal rejects the new concepts, assaulting them with the arguments of natural law, generously interspersing *mementote patres* throughout his harangue. He allows a pause; now a final thrust: "*Et de vexata pillula,*" he says into the silence, "*et de vexata pillula quam impropre catholicam dicunt*": "and now to that controversial pill which has been so improperly called Catholic." At this point, the address assumes the tone of a shout, takes wing, drives ahead, and reminds the fathers that any act against life may be a crime, can touch on homicide. At this very point, almost as if to emphasize the drama of the clash, the oration comes up against council rules. From a microphone, the voice of a moderator says drily: *"Rogatur orator ad conclusionem pervenire";* the orator is asked to conclude his address. Cardinal Ruffini interrupts himself immediately, adds two conclusions, and returns to his chair.

Cardinal Suenens now comes down from the grandstands to one of the microphones that stands on the first step of every section. Again in Latin, he slowly states the theses opposed to those of Cardinal Ruffini. It is a different type of oratory which rebuts the appeal to dogmatic morals by means of a more rationalized and relaxed ethical appeal to reason. Suenens enumerates the reasons that favor and those that contradict his thesis, and the assembly follows him in visible agreement. Many bishops make signs of approval from their benches as Suenens proceeds to finish his speech within the prescribed six minutes. When he ends, many hands rise as a sign of congratulation, and the bishops call back and forth expressing satisfaction. The tension of the debate falls after having reached a climax, and now less decisive communications are resumed.

Less expert voices follow at the microphone, and sentences begun in poor Latin terminate in Spanish or Dutch. But the bishops take notes, transcribe the new arguments for or against the subject under discussion. The voting is initiated and many fathers begin to write black crosses in the squares of "placet" (yes) or "non placet" (no) on the green perforated IBM-type cards used for voting. Others, less decided, come down from the grandstands to take walks and to consult with their colleagues. Some few go to pray in one of the chapels of St. Peter's. Now that the debate has become a fact, it takes on a different meaning despite the atmosphere of conflict that has pervaded it. It is at moments like this that we can see how improper it is to force layman's distinctions and political terms upon council sittings.

Naturally, I do not claim to speak of the council as a technician. Having been present there during one sitting means next to nothing. But my visit still remains a rapid impression of the cross section—the very center of the whirlpool of forces which are still shaking the Vatican. Some observations can be made that give some insight into certain of the council innovations. These innovations can hardly be understood apart from the meaning they had during their development. Our lay culture, so closely tied to the concept of "progressiveness," has decided that the council innovations were the outcome of a dialectical struggle between "progressives" and "conservatives." Recourse was taken to this simplification for various reasons, and not necessarily with any conscious intention of deforming facts; but the result is an ideological confusion disputed, up to the present, only by a handful of scholars.[3] The use of this terminology has made us think of the council as a struggle between adherents to or opponents of the idea of "progress" as it is commonly understood outside the Church. Meanwhile, the real "logic" of the council discussions was considerably different. This logic excluded the idea of "rupture" that outsiders attached to the council and it refuted a series of judgments on council "parliamentarism."

The impression I had was that of finding myself in an assembly similar to what seventeenth-century English assemblies must have been: brilliant, refined aristocratic gatherings of gentlemen in colorful Renaissance attire; but at the council above the attire were the clear and robust profiles of a ruling class that was not waiting for the passing of generations to carry their own experience into the Vatican. White, black, yellow faces, the physiognomies of proletarians, peasants, intellectuals, of southern and northern Europeans, of the Far East and of the New World—all bore witness to how conciliar exchanges came down to a vast series of concrete and widely varied experiences. When transferred outside of the discussion, outside its context, every address could present ideologically progressive or conservative lineaments. But in reality, each speech was born on the council floor as a pragmatic and concrete utterance or response to a living discussion. The orators I heard made their declarations on a personal basis, always repeating the phrase, "viewed from my diocese," "considered by my diocese." Or they made references to specific and individual experiences: "The laws of the country where we live," "the cultural base of our people." The image of a "decentralized centralism" among the bishops was not abstract in any way, so that the clashes, duels, and conflicts were pluralistic in nature, not prefabricated by the existence of two parties set up before and conditioning the encounter.

Similarly, the clashes and duels always expressed the same logical structure and often even the same "formal method." This was perfectly obvious to the observer. But whatever form this "pragmatic pluralism" took, it was always accompanied by much the same scheme of exposition, rooted in the same philosophy and method of thinking. But I won't dwell on this point. I only mention it to say that the odds and ends of the discussions that reached the outside world often lost this sense of philosophical unity, thus suggesting the presence of party politics of a modern and secular mold. In the same way, certain lay judgments concerning the "parliamentary technique" of the council discussions only remotely correspond to the reality inside. Admittedly, corridor maneuvering, strategy-conference strolls behind the naves, and the influence of pressure groups were present. But what was influential in the voting was less the lobbies or power groups than the best expressed and deepest forces of intelligence, which proved capable of giving a full and clear theological system to the pragmatism and experimentalism already mentioned. It is not a case of the progressives continuously registering majority votes; nor does it mean that Catholicism is mythically traveling progressive roads. The bishops whom we call "progressive" are leaders who prepared their addresses with the help of great theologians. Behind them was arrayed the intelligence of the world Church studying and surveying new terrains. As fate would have it, behind the few conservatives were only certain national churches (Spain and Italy) anchored in the official or curial theology, tied to sociological depressions, lacking cultural prestige, and representing, as one father put it, "the agricultural Church." Before every address, one could easily see the progressive leaders consulting with the Colombos and the Rahners. The fact is that the "aristocratic democracy" withdrew from the play of pressure groups linked to power positions, preferring to be motivated by considerations of another nature. Even those who were undecided and were waiting to hear how things developed were following logical and reasonable rules of play. Obviously, intelligence and cultural prestige in this way became pressure forces in their turn. But this is already a positive consideration; it tells us how such pressures were less bound to stimuli that we would like to qualify as "progressive" than to the intrinsic flux and continuity of Catholic thought, to the evolution of theology, and to the history of the Church.

The innovations of the council are therefore not the fruit of a clash between progressives and conservatives. The impression I had was that of seeing a battle between reformists and anti-reformists, thus continuing a well-known process. The discourse begun four centuries ago in the Council of Trent was being continued now in St. Peter's. "Reform" and "non-reform" were the real terms of the Catholic change. Like Trent, these terms naturally overlapped and defied any easy schematization. In Trent, the counterreform had generated the Catholic reform and vice versa.[4] In Trent, the reformist party wanted a reform as a step toward reaching an accord with the Protestants. The result was the creation of a counterreformist Church that assimilated from the Protestant movement those very reforming measures which gave it new impetus. Now, in the same way, the reforming discourse was begun again in Rome in different historical conditions and without counterreformist parties, but with antireformist currents. Among the reformists were arrayed the descendents of those Catholics who in the sixteenth century had sought an accord with the Protestants. At their side were those who wanted only to continue the Catholic "reform" begun in Trent. Here also were those currents which only a half century ago judged "modernism to be a heresy, though not in everything."[5] And though the variations were unlimited, the problem remained in fact one and the same, and that was not "progress," but Catholic reform. Here was a century-old problem which would receive unexpected solutions.

Three Flashbacks on the Council

My second memory of the council is of the seventh of December, 1965, the feast of St. Ambrose, patron of the pope's native Lombardy. It is the last council sitting; this time it is public. The day of reckoning has come. Within St. Peter's the atmosphere is completely different from before. The bishops and cardinals are in white. The "schismatics" have changed their places, mixing now with the diplomats and guests. Just after nine o'clock, Pope Paul VI makes his solemn entrance in a procession down the basilica nave, holding up the Gospel and then waiting on his throne for the council fathers to vote for the last time. From the height of the podium, the council secretary cries out in his Roman voice the titles of the schemata to be voted on. Then, while the electronic counting devices are making the last calculations, after thirty-seven months and twenty-seven days of work, after 168 plenary meetings, nine public sessions, and 548 votings, Paul VI celebrates the mass and delivers an address. And it is surely historic to hear this pope express "humanistic" thoughts in closing the first ecumenical council ever to end without condemnations, without anathemas, and without dogmas. "The Church of the Council," says the pope, "has been concerned not only with itself, but with man. . . . The whole of man who laughs and weeps, loves and thinks, has been standing, as it were, before the assembly of the Fathers throughout this council. And what took place here? A clash? A battle? An anathema? It could have come, but did not. Bear this in mind, you modern humanists, and acknowledge our new humanism. The value of the council is great because it declares itself in favor of and in the service of man. The Catholic religion and human life have reaffirmed here their eternal alliance."

After this address, Paul VI comes to the promulgation of the last four council documents. When he reads the approval of the decree on religious liberty, it is followed by the longest and most meaningful applause. Then, in utter silence, the equally historic joint declaration of the Catholic Church and the Orthodox Patriarchate of Constantinople is read, which revokes the reciprocal excommunications of the two Churches dating back to the year

1054. As the ancient anathemas are rescinded, the pope embraces the envoy of the Greek patriarch; there is a burst of applause for an event which has all the earmarks of concrete conciliation, just as the schema on religious liberty signifies a concrete affirmation of respect for the human conscience. Next to me, someone murmurs: "Now the Savonarola question should be straightened out."

The senior cardinal deacon finally invites the council fathers to rise and begins the final ceremony of closing the council: *"Date vobis pacem,"* he says—"bestow the kiss of peace." Every bishop embraces and kisses the one next to him as a sign of the end of debates and the healing of all discord. The pope, who had tenaciously upheld the schema on religious liberty and refused to anathematize atheists, slowly leaves the basilica in majestic procession.[6] The work of the Second Vatican Council has come to an end; amid an anachronistic burst of Renaissance ceremonial, a new age has begun.

As to the final significance of the council, it is too early to attempt a historical appraisal. At the closing of the Council of Trent four centuries before, no one could have predicted that that gathering would have given its name to a period of Church history; and just as "post-Tridentine Catholicism" was unforeseeable, so is "post-Vatican Catholicism" impossible to assess. Many decades will be required before the full significance of Vatican II is able to be discerned, and at this time even the most prudent conjecture seems somehow mere guesswork. Among the problems that will have to be resolved before adequate appraisal can be made are those of method. There is no doubt, for instance, that many judgments of the council smack of conciliar "triumphalism"—a transfer of the characteristic of absolute authority that Catholics used to apply to the Church, the bishops, and the pope, to a council that has demonstrated its strength, its freedom, and its capacity for renewal. One tends to regard as already "updated" a Church that has only just begun the painful process of updating itself. Even before the reforms are realized, it is taken for granted that the Church's "need of reform" will be followed by the emergence of a "reformed" Church. Meanwhile, there is also the skepticism of the mystical Catholics, who tend to overstress anti-triumphalism and to deny the validity of the positive judgments based on the results (i.e., religious liberty, institutional modifications) that can be measured by the yard-stick of history. The Church, they say, is not an inanimate object devoid of feeling. A Christian cannot reflect on the Church with-out reflecting on himself, and only he who has "real faith" can describe, and then only from within his own faith, what is taking place in the Church. This, however, is based on an unjustified claim. The fact is that the modern layman is criticized as soon as he begins to regard Catholicism as a great fact of history rather than as a perennial value. But this does not alter the fact that his observations may be very helpful toward understanding certain subtle Catholic developments that the mystical Catholic per-haps does not even notice. The mystic looks for "ruptures" and "shifts" like miracles, in much the same way that the Marxists or the leftist Catholics look for "revolutions."

In reality, we can make many observations on the council on the historical level above. We can assume, for example, that the council achieved many compromises. Probably, as one of its ex-perts has written, it did not produce even one decree that com-pletely satisfied the bishops.[7] Many documents are even "the fruit of logomachies." Very many are nothing more than the set-tlement of "a series of conflicts, uncertainties, and explorations." Hence, there also exists a council which is not a reform but a pure registration of how complex and intricate the problems were that the Church had accumulated over the years and how diffi-cult it is to be a witness of the Christian "message." Ambiguities, lacunae, and fears of reform come through time and again in the council documents. Diplomatic compromises were found to bridge the gap "between the majority that had the most vital theology for its ally, and the minority that controlled the machin-ery of the council"[8] on such subjects as collegiality, primacy, Scripture, and tradition. Nonetheless, even the severest critics hold that, in the midst of these obscurities, one can establish a perspective for the future by looking to the doors that were opened and the light that breaks through those open doors. Bearing this in mind, we can definitely evaluate the council as a neo-reform gathering. The Catholicism of Trent belongs decidedly to the past.

This book is not the place for an examination of the sixteen council documents,[9] but we can review quickly the main points that come to bear on a changing Vatican by reasoning as though we were looking at the proceedings of a constitutional convention. The Church of Rome has in fact accomplished a self-reform, a reform of its relations with other churches, of its judgments of other religions, and of its traditional positions with respect to the world. And the reform appears to be of vast scope, even if considered outside of the gradual applications that will derive from it. For example, Rome has given itself, for the first time in history, a constitution that defines the Church. The infallibility of the pope has been "reviewed," definitively establishing a collegiality of the bishops, which the Council of Trent had put aside. In initiating the ecumenical operation, *rapprochements* toward Protestants and other confessions were worked out which mean at least a revision of Tridentine principles. Without getting into theological details, several examples should suffice. The Church of Rome, the Church of hell and paradise, has begun to recognize as "Churches" certain other Christian groups which only yesterday were regarded as heretical communities. The "human conscience" and individual responsibility have been placed (along with the recognition of conscious procreation) at the center of Catholic life, whereas these concepts were previously rejected as Protestant. Contrary to Neo-Thomist prohibitions dating from the nineteenth century, the study of non-Scholastic philosophies is now being encouraged in seminaries. The laity is no longer dissuaded from reading the Bible as in the last century, and the Vulgate (the Latin translation for Catholics) is no longer proclaimed, as even Pius XII wished, as the only acceptable translation from the original texts. Conservative attacks notwithstanding, the methods of historical criticism have been explicitly approved, and it has been prescribed that Biblical studies must be the soul and foundation of all theology. The traditional Catholic positions on revelation have remained intact, to be sure, but the rest is clearly a question of soundly "anti-Tridentine" doctrinal innovation. Decentralization, "de-occidentalization," the internationalization of the Curia, the use of the vernacular in the liturgy, the end of an insistence upon absolute conformity with respect to the Oriental Churches, are all concepts which bring Catholicism fully into a spirit and development beyond Trent.

Other declarations go still further. There are some which definitely mean, as one theologian has written, a Catholic reconciliation with the ideas of the French Revolution which only yesterday were unconditionally condemned. Liberty, fraternity, and equality are in fact the keystones of the council doctrine concerning the Church and the modern world, toward the non-Christian religions, and toward atheists. In contrast to Trent and Vatican I, Rome has now repudiated the "medieval Catholic vision of the world" and integrated "classical theocentrism with a new humanism." This fundamental shift came with the recognition of religious liberty as the crucial point of future political developments and as the very essence of the neo-reform movement. Even though carefully worked over, the decree in fact proclaims that every man has the right to exercise religious liberty, that every religious community has the right to liberty, that every state, every society, every church has the duty of defending this liberty. Similarly, the document on "The Church and the Modern World" marks another basic departure. Contrary to the "Syllabus" of a century earlier that condemned such "modern ideas" as religious liberty and the notion of progress, the council has proclaimed a new and radically positive, even if not undiscriminating, attitude toward progress. It has fully endorsed the rights of man and the principles of dignity and freedom, substituting a dialogue with the contemporary world in place of the polemic, cooperation instead of disapproval. It is not a case of general ideas tied to a superficial show of secularization, as many lay conservatives would have it. The council affirms the principle of freedom for cultural creations, scientific research, even for theological studies. Aside from the compromises made on the theories of a "just war," it abandons the Church's ancient diffidence toward international organizations and subscribes to supernational cooperation on the problem of peace. Without anathemas, an attempt is being made to define atheism as a "cultural form."

All of this takes on even vaster significance when we evaluate the judgments formulated with respect to non-Christian religions. The revoking of the condemnation of Jews, the recognition of the spiritual, moral, and cultural values in the Buddhist, Mohammedan, and other world religions, open up a vista beyond all expectations. When we recall the anti-Semitic decisions of the Fourth Lateran Council and the traditional denial of the "grains of truth" contained in non-European religions, we begin to sense the significance of these innovations. We can deduce from all this that many problems still pending will be resolved by future generations reared in respect for liberty, in the cult of the human conscience, with a taste for collegiality—solutions which were never reached in the religion of authority. Many things either denied or feared by earlier councils were courageously codified or formulated. The Copernican laws of the new Catholicism have been written and promulgated.

It disturbs Catholics to speak of the French Revolution, of Copernican laws and the Catholic renewal as if it were all a question of the victory of modern culture finally managing to produce a crisis of conscience and compunction in the Church of Rome. At the same time, a "neo-reform" which is apparently assimilating various Protestant and modernist positions tends to inflate anti-Catholics. We are told by some that brotherhood, equality, and liberty were Christian terms. Others tell us that freedom and conscience are the idols of disobedient Catholics. But if we overcome our fear of words, if we know the exact Catholic position toward modernism, if we admit the presence within Catholicism of an autonomous spirit of reform marked by failures and successes, advances and retreats, then every polemical tendency will fall for lack of a real foundation. The last important declaration of the council was, in fact, an assurance of "permanent reform." We can extinguish all our pride and anxieties in the *Ecclesia semper reformanda*—the perennially self-reforming Church. In the autonomy of the "reform," Catholicism is reassimilating values it once produced and gave to the world. And such are the great values of freedom and equality, values which were born in the Church but which left it for the arena of modern political history. They are the values of the human conscience that survived the Protestant and modernist crisis.

Quite naturally, there are many perplexing things about this "Catholic humanism." Many think that the council lost the Johannine impetus with which it opened,[10] and that when the final showdown came, it went on to produce only a series of major failures. The most noticeable of these was the expected total condemnation of war that the council should have made but never did. We cannot regard this failure as of little consequence because it will inevitably affect either the development of the political ideology of Catholicism or the diplomatic relations of the Vatican with other states. It was, in fact, a question of establishing principles capable of hindering repetitions of past provocations (the blessing of artillery by the clergy, the theology of the "just war," military decorations for chaplains, etc.) and capable of preventing future undesirable actions (the blessing of atomic arsenals). But the "Gospel" solution—the dedication of the Roman Church to practice actively those principles of nonviolence contained in its preaching—was not formally articulated. Even such "conservative" cardinals as Ottaviani, a man of the Holy Office and leader of the "non-reformers," had called for a firm and definitive pronouncement, with his now famous sentence *"Bellum omnino interdicendum"*—"every type of war must be forbidden." But the debate ended in a compromise, and the return to the casuistry of the "just war" and the "defensive war" will perpetuate the neutralism of many Catholics and the anti-neutralism of others, for no one who declares war ever admits to being the aggressor. The condemnation of war the council did eventually proclaim was so severe toward the arms race and so freighted with pacifism that it only paves the way for subtle dispute, opportunistic justification, and political controversy. Whether Catholic or not, all heads of governments can find there the legitimization of all their acts. The national Churches that are so powerful today can—like the national episcopates of yesterday—justify reversible alliances and chauvinistic benedictions on the basis of this document. Thus, in the context of the other resolutions, this council failure has serious dimensions.

The failures relating to other social questions deserve a different treatment. Some basic and concrete problems of modern man—e.g. divorce, birth control—were also left unsolved, thus forming another "double finale" at the council. In this area, we may note a discrepancy between the new and unprecedented positions taken by the Church in the area of major ideas and the suggested "guidelines for action" touching on the burning problems of contemporary society. There is, for instance, a glaring difference between the council's rich and daring ideological humanism and its social humanism, which is filled with compromises. The problems were considered and were "postponed"— which means that they were entrusted to the decisions of the pope and his successors. Many therefore look like algebraic equations with several unknown factors, which consequently can admit of several solutions.[11] Such is the case with birth control which, if it had been resolved in terms of a "Catholic pill," would have satisfied certain "council expectations" but would have shifted Catholic emphasis from *authoritarian procreation* to *authoritarian limitation.* On the premises of *conscious procreation,* meanwhile, other solutions are left open. On the whole, this failure obviously takes on another meaning when it is presented simply as a postponement. The intention of the council in this area was to leave the future open, and future popes will have behind them a modern council that preferred a blank page to condemnations and anathemas. The shape of the post-Vatican period can be seen even in these lacunae which while they may not favor a new Catholic trend, still do not block it.

From such a council is born a changing Vatican. We need only read what historians tell us of the predecessor Councils of Trent and Vatican I to appreciate what happened at Vatican II.[12] In the Council of Trent, "the hoped-for accord with Protestants failed completely because of the comportment of Protestants themselves and because the council formulated all the controversial dogmatic points according to rigidly Catholic doctrine." Hence "ecclesiastical tradition was declared to be a foundation of faith alongside Scripture. Moreover, the ecclesiastical authority was declared to be the only competent interpreter of Scripture. And the Catholic sacramental system was definitively confirmed." Then "there was a battle between an episcopalistic current that saw the power of episcopal jurisdiction as deriving directly from Christ, and the curialistic current which maintained it derived from the pope. No decision was reached. Still, the triumph of papal authority was in practice confirmed because the council was directed and controlled by papal legates." As to Vatican Council I and Pius IX's "Syllabus of Errors" that preceded it, "the pope came out as the absolute director of the consciences of the world." The "Syllabus" and the encyclical *Quanta cura* "condemned the principle of the religious neutrality of States, the principle of freedom of opinion and the press, the principle of absolute popular sovereignty, the principle of the juridical supremacy of the State over the Church." They forbade "religious freedom, every accommodation of the Church with progress, liberalism, and modern civilization," the result being "an anathema on all the ideas of the century." One may willingly admit the thesis of Catholic continuity and "immutable permanence." But this thesis also permits us to say that a period which lasted four hundred years has now come to an end. The change was too great not to consider that a second Reformation was under way. We cannot foresee what it will bring, and perhaps it is wrong to call it that. But at least we can call the years lying before us the "post-Vatican" period.[13]

My third memory of the council goes back to the morning of December 8, 1965. We are in the big square outside St. Peter's basilica for the open-air ceremony that is to put Vatican Council II definitively behind us. Everything is very formal and spectacular this time, and an unchanging Vatican seems to have been resurrected for the occasion. Discourses, fanfares, the pope on his throne, gala dress, priests with high-powered lenses on their cameras taking pictures even during the Elevation of the Mass, contented monsignori who are going "back home," Roman nobility in Renaissance pantaloons and swords, Swiss cavalry, papal sergeants, Roman princes-assistants at the papal court, and finally the reading of the decree formally closing the council. But while this was going on, and gray clouds were racing across the Roman sky, one could observe the mass of 2500 council fathers undiminished by schism or by any irreparable discords. Observers of every confession and every sect were present, and ninety representatives from ninety nations, Yugoslavia and Israel included, paid their homage and respect to the present papacy. There was even a certain symbolism in this ceremony—not unlike that expressed by Pope Paul's conferences with such intellectuals and artists as Maritain, Nervi, Ungaretti, or his meetings with workers in overalls, with the sick, and with children of six continents—a symbolism that testified to an evidently genuine program of pacification and reconciliation. The whole presented a serene finale to a council that closed with the genuine esteem of all confessions and with the respect of the majority of states. Such things elicited a series of thoughts in at least one individual who witnessed this spectacle.

One recalled reading how Vatican Council I closed in 1870; that it never really came to an end, but was interrupted by discord among the bishops and by the distrustful anxiety of national governments in a turbulent and exasperating period. One recalled certain chronicles, such as that of Vitelleschi Nobili,[14] which recorded anything but a happy finale to that council. Even the weather, with lightning and thunder instead of the bright Italian sun, seemed to accent the misfortune that marked the violent breakup of the council. Against this sinister background of a Rome that "seemed to bring tidings of ill-starred events" had moved, a century before, the protagonists of a convulsive phase of history. The pope, Pius IX, was infallible but unhappy. The vehemence of those opposed to infallibility had provoked more than a hundred bishops to desert the council. The other Christian Churches, though absent from the council, realized that the new dogmas widened, rather than narrowed, the gulf separating them from Roman Catholicism. Lay opinion reacted violently, and with heated polemics, to the decision of the papacy to define itself as an absolute monarchy, regarding that definition as a reaction against the liberal tendencies then transforming the face of Europe. And as a conclusion to all this, the council ended in the dissatisfaction of many Catholics, the flight from Rome of the fathers of the "liberal" faction, and the presence of only five or six diplomatic delegations. There were also such disconcerting events as the rupture of the Austrian Concordat, Vienna claiming to have concluded it with a "different" sovereign. In 1965, the circumstances were exactly the opposite of those on that morning in 1870.

Different circumstances and a different moment of history had occasioned that earlier council. But the chronicles of the times registered the positive and negative aspects with glaring objectivity. It was Vitelleschi Nobili who wrote: "The Church's need to organize itself more as a monolith on the principle of authority is understandable to everyone. Organized in that way, the Catholic Church is certainly easier to govern and its full weight is more easily brought to bear in the political and social struggles of the day. But, putting theological considerations aside and only considering the social and civil circumstances connected with a question of this dimension and the practical results that society can derive from the influence of the Vatican Council, we must make certain objections. It can be said that with such an organization and structure, everything that is intelligent, rational, and liberal in Catholicism, finding itself constantly more constrained within this circle, will always tend to withdraw from it and will in fact easily find itself outside it in a wider and more rational circle, a circle more favorable to an opposition to that irrational center, a circle in which the irresistible movement of modern life has all the space it needs to traverse its orbit unimpeded." And this was the thinking that divided the council fathers, made national governments withhold their consent, and drove religious persons of other confessions from Vatican Council I.

To understand why the present council closed, by contrast, with such felicitous manifestations, we should reconsider these words of Nobili. The ninety diplomatic delegations, the numerous non-Catholic observers, the concord of the council fathers, the attention of the lay world, are in fact the exact reversal of the situations and conditions of 1870. In three years of discussion, the Catholic Church of our day saw fit to make different choices. Instead of "organizing itself in a tight circle," it has broadened its own sphere, extending its scope and its boundaries, thereby creating the conditions for a different relationship with the world, with Catholics themselves, with separated Christian confessions, with thitherto "accursed" religions such as Judaism. The chroniclers of the last century would never have forecast such a revolutionary step for a Church "organized on authority." Yet, this is precisely what happened. Meanwhile, considering the "civil and social implications" of the council, "the tracing of a larger and more rational circle" has been made, "a circle more capable of containing modern life."

To those who ask why this has happened, to those who want a simple explanation without technical subtleties, an answer has been given. There is no doubt at all that the cause of all the hopes, the agreements and the auspicious conclusions can be found in one word; and that word is liberty. No council from Nicea and Chalcedon to Trent ever tried so hard as this council to understand the rationale of human liberty. No previous councils ever used so freely the two words that are so basic in the life of man. The three years of the council were filled with signs of respect for freedom of conscience, with a desire to bring about concord among the various confessions, with honest attempts to understand the doubts of those who do not believe. Naturally, some expectations met with disappointment. But the logic of the general agreement is obvious to all. The council was able to produce positive results only because, in proclaiming the rights of liberty, the council fathers and the pope made use of the very liberty to which they were committing the Church. The council schemata, which in the beginning were predominantly arid and curial, were in fact courageously worked over, reshaped, and reformed by the non-curial bishops. Some of these changes were less than efficacious, but for the most part they were given new and daring forms that provoked the revolution of which we have spoken. The open discussions, and the absence of powerful majorities set up in advance, permitted a slow and continuous process of osmosis between progressives and conservatives, thus avoiding the formation of vast static and irreducible minorities.

The only council document that had a thin majority was the Decree on Social Communications. The others, all of more fundamental importance, were all passed with more than 2200 or 2300 votes out of about 2350 council fathers. And this permitted the council to make the principles of freedom and charity triumph without inflexibilities and ruptures, without reservations of any significance. Wisely, Paul VI did not use the weight of his authority to limit the use of council freedom, not even when the "council fathers rejected certain schemata" (such as the "Schema on the Missions") that had previously been publicly approved by the pontiff. Thus, we may say that freedom was respected and proclaimed by the council as one of man's great endowments, and precisely because the council fathers themselves exercised that gift day by day with a modern consciousness, discovering its immense value more and more as their work progressed.[15]

The words "freedom," "tolerance," the "respect" for different freedoms, for different beliefs, etc., are found time and again in all the council documents—sometimes in veiled and carefully phrased expressions, and at times in subtle and legalistic terms to be sure, but still solemn and definitive enough to guarantee results. And the new positions of the Church received clear confirmation in the words which Paul VI spoke in the Sistine Chapel to the representatives of states and governments, from every nation and continent of the earth. As the theme of his greeting on this highly significant occasion, the pope chose freedom. And probably never in history were a pope's words so precise in exalting such a great value in moral life. The pope said first: "In the declarations on the non-Christian religions, the Church invites us to consider the positive values contained in all beliefs, and it is easy to appreciate the true benefits that can result from such a consideration for social peace." And then he went on, explaining in these words the document on religious freedom: "Let no one be forced to believe; and likewise, let no one be hindered from believing. Whatever be in fact the judgment one might make about historical situations that took place in the past of certain nations, today the Church asks for herself nothing more than the freedom of announcing the Gospel."

Thus, when everything was finished and consigned to history, such was the commitment made by the pope before the representatives of the powers that maintain relations with the Holy See; it was obviously addressed as well to all other nations. Apparently these were "the influences of the council for human society" and the reason for the interest that surrounded the council since its beginning. It is pointless to ask ourselves whether this position of the Church of Rome was a belated or forced "discovery" of freedom. What really counts is that in her dialogue on both ethical and civil planes—and hence in her dialogue with history—the Church has made this affirmation of a value which until then had been deprived of her support. This was the major achievement of the council.

The council, by means of its "commissions," is in fact continuing to work at the present time.[16] These commissions constitute a permanent council which, in certain cases, outlives Vatican II. They make possible further adaptations, innovations, and modifications without awaiting the change of generations. To be sure, the Church is not a society into which one can introduce a mechanical concept of cause and effect. After the "constitutional convention," there is no constitutional court to guarantee the carrying of the new ideas over into practice. It is said that a "council begins when a council ends." But is this true, and if so, how true? Catholics, non-Catholics, and governments want to know whether the reality of the council continues now that Vatican II has ended and the bishops have gone home. If it does, under what forms; and where? If the council has indeed given us reason to think that the Vatican is changing, it should be possible to answer these questions.

CHAPTER II

A Talk with Pope Paul VI

Pope Paul VI received me in his private library the evening before his trip to the UN, and spoke mainly about the Vatican today. He conversed slowly and with great frankness about the Church, the council, Italy, Church-state relations in Italy, and his visit to the United Nations. As is known, popes do not grant interviews; they have never done so. But my conversation with Pope Paul developed out of a visit to the pope which was itself marked by simple casualness and not by anything official, out of a meeting that was as uncommon as it was casual. I went to the second loggia about seven o'clock, the hour at which audiences end and the lights in the apostolic palaces are put out. Paul VI was standing behind a long walnut table, and he moved toward the door with the naturalness and gestures of a modern man capable of rapid human relations. Against the background of the books and in the clear light of the salon cleared of gold trim and baldachins, the pope put out his hand without in any way imposing or soliciting the kiss of the ring. Then he began scanning the armchairs around the table until he seemed to have found the one that was most comfortable and nearest to his desk. "Over here," he said, "you sit there, and we'll be able to talk better." It didn't seem to be a mere gesture of courtesy, but rather an explicit renunciation of the classic, and traditional, monologue of popes.

On the other side of his desk, Paul's white figure made a unique picture. He sat there holding a letter opener in his hands. The lamp made his robe and mantle sparkle, and under the table I caught a glimpse of his red pontifical slippers. I was looking at a relaxed man, a spontaneous man, a man very different from the severe and rather tense pope one somehow expects; and he seemed anything but the introverted, nervous, and diplomatic pope of the journalists.

"You know, it's a pleasure to talk about the Vatican," the pope said immediately, with a congenial expression on his face. "Many are studying us today, trying to understand us. Many books have come out on the Holy See and the council; and some are good, too. But many put thoughts into the Church's mind without ever having bothered to ask the Church what she really does think on certain matters. And, after all, our opinion should also count in religious questions." The pope paused here, almost with delight in what he had just said. Then he cut his smile short, and went on: "But we are aware that it's not easy to understand what is being done and discussed in the world of the Church. You know, even the pope sometimes has trouble understanding today's Church."

After this informal and frankly human preamble, Paul VI turned to the most important questions of his pontificate. In the evening stillness of that salon, he unhesitatingly took up the most difficult and critical subjects, and he did it as a man of our time —as one who doesn't set out to evade anything, obviously speaking out of a sincerity that flatly refuses to take the easy way out. Without writing (it is not permitted to write in the presence of the popes), I made an effort to engrave his sentences word for word in my memory as he spoke, not hiding his sad realism, of the Church and the world, of the dialogue, of his succession to John XXIII.

"One has to be both simple and circumspect at the same time," he told me, "to grasp the meaning of the years we are living in. The Church wants to become multilateral so as better to reflect the contemporary world. To do this, she has decided to drive the plow into inert terrain, even into the hardest ground, in order to move and vivify and bring to light what lay buried there. This plowing causes unrest, strainings and problems. It was our predecessor's task to sink the plow into the soil. Now the task of driving it ahead has fallen into our hands."

At this point, Paul VI stopped. He placed his hands on top of the desk and looked at them for a moment, as if he were bothered by their fragility. But then he hid them immediately, almost as if from a sudden sense of modesty, and passed on, with the same vivid realism I have mentioned, to utterances that showed him clearly to be a modern pope, a pope incapable of illusions.

"Many people are wondering," he said, "why the Church goes to all this trouble. They wonder what the dialogue is supposed to accomplish. But they ask these things only because they are not conscious of the real problem. The real problem is that the Church is opening up to the world only to find a world that for the most part isn't open to the Church. St. Charles Borromeo, for example, lived under very different conditions in Milan. When I was in Milan"—Paul VI forgot the papal "we" for a second—"I saw records of the diocese dating back to Borromeo's time. The problems were the acquisition of a confessional, the repair of a church, the presence of thee drunks in a parish, the matter of a prostitute. But how different things are today. Today it's no longer a question of a prostitute in the parish. It's a question of millions of persons who have no religious belief. This is why the Church has no choice but to open up. We have to meet the person who doesn't believe any more, who doesn't believe in us. We have to meet him head on and say to him: 'This is what we are; this is how we are built. Now, tell us why you don't believe, why you fight us.'" And here the pope interrupted himself. He seemed to be trying to erase the sadness that this view of things was tracing on his face. His own simplicity came to his assistance. "And so, we have the dialogue," he concluded, resuming his smile. "That's the whole secret, you see."

This talking and explaining oneself freely, this desire to keep the interlocutor from feeling isolated, this continuous circumvention of the barriers that naturally arise between a layman and a pope, this refusal to abandon himself to cant, this ceaseless preoccupation for the interest of the other person, seems to me a basic side of Paul VI's character. In the features of his face I could read the unmistakable consciousness that a modern pope must take on the risk of direct, mobile, and humanly acceptable discourse. But this will come out in the rest of the conversation, which was always absolutely frank and in no way "rehearsed." The pope moved on, as a matter of fact, to those delicate points which often occasion criticism of his pontificate, such as the council, the conflict between progressives and conservatives, his posture vis-à-vis the Curia, the so-called flagging of ecumenism, and other matters.

Paul VI went on: "This dialogue and this new posture of the Church are certainly giving rise to discussions inside the Church, with the result that the Vatican has become the center of world attention. But the true problem is still what we said before: the Church in a world that for the most part is losing belief. As for other things, you know, we have to consider them in their true proportions. If nothing else, the council showed that there is fortunately no Church crisis paralleling the world's crisis of faith. Even the most serious subjects of the day like religious freedom were debated on all sides with love for the Church. And I don't have to tell you what this world problem means."

The pope paused, underlining with silence this "liberal" problem of his pontificate. Then he went on: "The forming of two sides, progressives and non-progressives, as they say, never raises the problem of fidelity. They are all discussing for the good of the Church, and there were neither defections nor disturbing indications of internal struggle. If there had been, as many say there were, the pope would have been concerned, you know, and he would have spoken out. That, after all, is why there is a pope!"

When he said that, Paul VI had pointed with an expression of humor to the chair he was sitting on. And then he moved on in this vein of spontaneous humor. Often criticized as a defender of the Curia, the pope was not hesitant to speak on this matter. "Many problems," he said, "are distorted by remoteness. But discussion simplifies them. Take the discussions about the Curia, for example—you know, all those accusations of 'centralism' and 'Romanism.' But now the problem is taking on its true dimensions. It was enough to come to Rome to see that the Church is in much better health now than she used to be, and that certain defects are not as dramatic as they first seemed."

These words seemed to reflect Paul VI's experience as a former Substitute Secretary of State, as "technician" of the Church. He gave himself to explanations gladly, and rapidly. "In the past, the Church was dominated by kings and emperors, whereas today she is free, and the pope thinks as he likes. In the past, there was nepotism, which no longer exists. In the past there were cases of simony, and now there is certainly nothing of the kind. As you know, even Curia members were known to commit simony in the past. And do you know why? It often happened that in order to finance themselves, the Curia made people pay for the documents they were requesting. But today the Roman Curia receives regular salaries, as do good civil servants all over the world. Of course, certain technical reforms are called for to make the Curia function more efficiently. There will always be personnel matters that need to be taken care of. But no really grave problems are involved. If there were, it would be our concern to solve them. Do you think the pope would deny the evils of the Vatican government if they were there? He would draw up a list of them, study them, and eliminate them." Again Paul VI was smiling, enjoying the pleasure of an objective discourse, like a technician talking about a mechanism that he knows perfectly; but speaking also as a pope who does not categorically defend

the curial line, and who only wants to continue the demythologizing of the facts begun by the council itself.

Caught, as it were, in this state of mind, in this human key, he
went on to talk of ecumenism. "The council served to simplify
many things," he said, "even considered as the encounter of men
from different Churches. Did you see the observers at the council? Those of Athenagoras [the Greek patriarch] were missing, as
we all know. But the others came, and now they know us. No
one has taken any decisive steps yet, of course. We shouldn't
fool ourselves. But the atmosphere has definitely changed. For
example, one day a Waldensian came with the observers to see
us. He appeared at the door, came toward us reaching out his
hand, and said: 'How are you? We haven't seen each other for
five hundred years.'" And Pope Paul laughed openly.

Paul VI let a few seconds pass, as if to permit a question, and
then the conversation switched over to his visit to the UN. But
here too his words were in a way colored by humor and a smile.
To be sure the pope's visit to the UN has given rise to numerous
discussions of his "activism" and his intervention in international
politics. But Paul VI spoke of the subject with simplicity. As a
matter of fact, his discourse had become so natural that he was
talking now with obvious North Italian inflections.

On his trip to the UN, Paul VI said this: "Oh, yes, oh yes. We
are going to make this trip. They asked us to come to celebrate
the twentieth anniversary of the UN and we answered that we
would. The pope can hardly say: 'Thanks very much, but I'm too
busy.' As far as we are concerned, we'd just as soon not go, so
as to save the money and trouble it will cost everyone. But for the
first time, the heads of the whole world are meeting and want to
hear the word of Christ's representative, and so we can't refuse
to make this trip. So we will put on a pilgrim's coat. Believe me,
it will be St. Rocco's coat, it will be as St. Rocco that we go
there."

Saying this, the pope shook his head. He seemed suddenly to
be the man pushing seventy who is crushed by the human effort
it takes to do certain things. But this time too, discretion and

modesty immediately reversed the fallen and sad expression in his eyes. He rejected this pathetic image with readiness and corrected it immediately with a smile: "We have to do as the psalm says, you know: *Loquebar in conspectu regum et non confundebar;* 'I will speak before kings, and will not be confused.' But who knows if we will succeed in doing as well as we would wish before so many important people?"[1]

The golden clock on the pope's table struck again. But Paul VI did not rise. He had welcomed a question on Italy and he went right into it, without rhetoric and circumstantial expressions; even into the thorny area of state-Church relations: "They always ask us for a word on Italy," he said, "but it is so hard to know what to say. If we speak out, someone claims that the pope intervenes in Italian affairs. If we don't speak out, they say that the pope doesn't have the courage to say what he thinks. On occasion, of course, we have intervened. But we only did so because religious and moral problems required it. However, that doesn't mean that the pope is in favor of intervention, or that he wants to treat Italian Catholics differently from other Catholics. From *here*, we definitely don't recommend any one political line in preference to another."

Paul VI had placed his hand on the table, saying "here" with decisiveness. Then, he wanted to go on to remove all possible ambiguity from what he had said. "Italy, Italy," he said with emotion. But in the fear of being rhetorical, he repressed even the feeling of affection welling up in him, and instead chose the difficult path of the direct statement. "Many things are not easy," he said, "but perhaps good will can most help the Italians. The way is trying, but there's no need to lose heart. You see, at the bottom of it the problem is a moral one. There has been progress. New roads have been built, etc. But maybe the advance in men's hearts hasn't kept the same pace and—how shall I say it?—under the surface something is corroding and dividing them. But I don't want to say any more on this. It's so easy to misconstrue the words of a pope about Italy."

But Paul VI did not stop. The problem of state-Church relations had now become the theme of his talk and he wanted to cut right through to the heart of the matter. And this he did with the sadness of his realism and with the humility of a scientist who never shirks a problem. "We are in a delicate position," he told me. "State and Church, Church and state. This relation is particularly difficult because of our being in Italy. We know that our presence in Italy causes a problem for Italian life. We know this, believe me. At times we are a stumbling block, even to those who like us." Then the pope stopped to think, putting a note of sincere humanity into an old political subject. "But we have to find a solution," he continued. "We have to earn each other's respect. Each must stay in his own field. We want the Italians to live their political life freely. We constantly advise our priests not to mix in nonreligious questions, not even to ask about them, not to travel paths on which they don't belong." Stretching out his arms, as if better to express his feeling of resignation, he went on to conclude: "But we live on the same soil and the overlapping of daily life often contradicts our general policy. Oftentimes it is inconvenient for the Church to have her feet on earth."

At this point, Paul VI was obviously preparing to bring our talk to a close. But then he suddenly seemed to change his mind. He preferred a last reflection on the problem of birth control, in a way summarizing its historical position with his lucid simplicity. "So many problems!" he said, almost as if speaking to himself. "How many problems there are and how many answers we have to give! We want to open up to the world, and every day we have to make decisions that will have consequences for centuries to come. We have to respond to the questions of the man of today, the Christian of today, and there are some questions that are particularly difficult for us, such as those connected with the problem of the Christian family." Then the pope's realism became especially vivid. "Take birth control, for example. The world asks what we think and we find ourselves trying to give an answer. But what answer? We can't keep silent. And yet, to speak is a real problem. The Church hasn't had to deal with such things for centuries. And it is a somewhat foreign and even humanly embarrassing subject for men of the Church. So, the commissions meet, the reports pile up, the studies are published. Oh, they study a lot, you know. But then we still have to make the final decisions. And in deciding, we are all alone. Deciding is not as easy as studying. We have to say something. But what? God will simply have to enlighten us."

My colloquy with Paul VI ended with those words. I should try to describe the impression it left with me (naturally omitting the emotions that such a human experience elicits). I could call it a "prologue," a prologue to my visit and a prologue to the changing Vatican. But I prefer to consider it differently. I prefer not to attribute too much significance to that "self-portrait" quality which comes through from the talk and which modifies considerably the most common images of the pope. Being John XXIII's successor definitely gave birth to all kinds of comparisons between Paul and John. Hence, the ever recurring contrast of congeniality vs. rigorousness, joyfulness vs. Hamletism, extroversion vs. anguish, and hence the inevitable deductions regarding their respective methods of governing the Church, again reduced to such fixed formulae as open vs. closed, open dialogue vs. controlled dialogue, progress vs. stasis. But my talk with Paul VI only points up the inexactitude and uselessness of such psychological interpretations. Paul VI was in good health, tanned, even mellowed in the physical features of age. If anything, these were clear indications of how unfaithful and abused official photography and television are in Italy, which in this case only succeed in showing Paul VI as tense, cold, pallid, and anything but spontaneous. His spirit didn't seem to me to be obsessed by nightmares and neuroses, but to be humorous and free. What many take for anguish seemed to me reflectiveness. What many have defined as Hamletism seemed to me healthy circumspection and the flexibility that realism implies. I would call Paul VI a man of his time, a man not interested in the facile expression and the favorable reaction of the moment, but in the discourse valid in itself and in results which will grow to their fruition in due season. He is a man who is aware that his office means lone-

liness, doubt, contradiction, questioning, and requires the courage it takes to express such things; a pope who is familiar with
the historical situation in which he is moving and who lives it
with secret excitement.

To be sure, these are only impressions. And I should not want
to reduce him to simply another psychological type, which would
be to commit the same fault I myself object to. If I did, everything I said would be held suspect, and justly so. I would be
accused of repaying his courtesy with a sort of "Pauline paternal-
ism" or the usual "personality cult" one so easily pays to popes.
Many Catholics, even priests, have accused me of dancing to
Paul VI's tune, pointing to the absence from my writings of the
usual accusations levied against him. Militant Catholicism is full
of battles of this kind. I prefer not to enter into this typically
clerical discussion between the "Johannites" and the "Paulites."

I would say rather that such a conversation is helpful in seeing
the figure of Paul VI as a personality representative of our time,
as the interpreter of a historical moment which prolongs, and at
the same time ceases to be, that of Pope John XXIII. His words
on state and Church definitely identify him as a "liberal" pope;
they even seem to suggest a new way of understanding concordat politics. His policy of continuity with respect to John XXIII
is certainly no secret. His way of viewing religious problems
without arrogance or undue optimism reflects a responsible,
cautious, and dramatic realism, as even certain radical observers
have recognized. His "curialism" is a fact, but it is more of a
technical than a political nature. His renowned "efficiency cult"
is certainly a commitment to the necessities of an age, besides
being the result of his character. But especially clear is his desire
to commit the Church, without false enthusiasm and without
neotriumphalism, to the post-conciliar age. Paul VI gave me the
impression that he knows what it means to be pope in such a
delicate phase of history as ours, clearly refusing the intransi-
gence of Pius IX toward reformist currents, but also resisting the
temptation to "progressive" superiority typical of our century.
Having been progressive as a cardinal, perhaps he is familiar with

a well-known thought of Simone Weil: "It is essential to know how to change sides and to be like justice, ever escaping before the victors, wherever they come from." His character is certainly inclined to indecision. But it is not "Hamletism." If anything, it is the desire for balance and "flight" before the very victories he likes.

In substance, there are two facts that characterize Paul VI's government. Paul is a cautious pope rather than a contradictory pope. What he is pursuing now, as in the council, is the continuous search for majority decisions. His flexibility is political, then, not psychological, and it tends, with the give-and-take technique and the slow decision, to move forward in the unity and with the consent of the majority. Hence, there is a continuous back-and-forth movement between opposite positions (which often disappoints and displeases), between winners and losers. But he apparently has a clear vision of his role, and he fulfills that role, accepting all its consequences and all criticism. Now that the fifties—the years of the glorious pronouncements—are over, we must face the difficult sixties.

The pontificate of Paul VI is the first definitely to be characterized by the council, and so is quite distinct from that of John XXIII, which opened everything up without experiencing the problems of that opening. After having accepted the "pluralism of the modern world," the Church now has to interpret that pluralism and set up a "plurality of instruments." Thus, with the council and the delicate creative phase it represented all behind us, another phase has begun. And it is not Paul VI's duty merely to translate the new ideas into action. What he has to do is to "create" those orientations that the council left undefined, and to see that the council decisions are not used to bring about a crystallization similar to that which followed Trent. It is the age of the Catholic Church committed to the permanent evolution. It is the age of a pontiff who represents in himself the margin of the Church's incompleteness, the Church's provision against unforeseen hours of difficulty, her post-conciliar reserve in an era hardly begun. Ours is an age of rectification, an age of resetting, an age of gradual adaptation. And it is the joyless age of long-term decisions, an age that cannot be judged day by day; it is an age far from Pacellian or Johannine certainties. Such is the phase that Paul VI is directing. He wants it so with all his will. But, at the same time, as Hegel might say, he is the interpreter of a process that is greater than his power.

For this reason, however others view it, my talk with Paul VI did not strike me as a "prologue." As it often happens in traveling, certain images impress themselves upon the memory, summarizing a situation and establishing a direct contact with the world one wishes to discover. Such was the contact I experienced while conversing with Pope Paul. I realize I am hereby calling down upon myself the scorn of the Johannites. I know I am swimming against the current. Perhaps what I am saying will not even please the very pontiff whose guest I was. His conclusions on the council are well known. His distinctions on the Vatican, which registers not "change" but "renewal," are philosophically exact in not admitting an unjustifiable "qualitative" philosophic jump. Then there are certainly cautious, disputed, and at times troubling positions in Paul VI's pontificate. Still, it was before his image (and I would say in spite of his image) that I seemed to have a tangible and direct contact with a historical reality that outstrips the very logic that tries to analyze it: the image of a thin pope, with his crude gothic profile, resigning himself to Catholicism as a minority position because "the reality is that the world doesn't believe any more"; his gently cold look that asks, "We have to say something, but what?" This image seemed perfect for focusing our attention on the changing Vatican.

For Catholicism, the Vatican does not change; by its own definition, it is only "renewed." But in renewing itself, it has reached certain frontiers beyond which even that which the council's directives seem to have stabilized through definition becomes mobile and questioning, a continually recurring hypothesis. The force of the *aggiornamento* was such that even extreme questions were raised. And throughout my trip to the Vatican, this meeting with Paul VI was to remain in my memory as the key to the changing Vatican, as the code for deciphering a world which, though it has admittedly not theorized "qualitative jumps," has registered such a profound shift that it is conscious of having come to the limits of its very being. Perhaps future events will prove the contrary to be true. But when moments like this occur in history, prefabricated systems of logic collapse.

The simplest moments of an experience are being lived and one senses something like a feeling of relief pervading the world of discreet monsignori, learned theologians, and able diplomats. The circumspect figure of Paul VI is committing a closed and theocratic society to the risky business of a prolonged overture to the world, and this in spite of the perplexities and doubt that such an overture implies. It is in fact at moments like these that the Vatican appears as a world still only half made and dangerously exposed to the vagaries of time and man, a world open in a Christian way to the indeterminate factors of history. It is a Vatican which contrasts with the determinism of the lay world of our day, a Vatican which also contrasts with its own determinism of yesterday, a Vatican that was consumed, worn down and smoothed by centuries, but which is now freighted, unexpressed, fermenting, pregnant with questions. They are questions that seek out, with man himself, "the link that does not hold."[2] This Catholicism that asks and declares itself to be unsure in the very voice of a pope, in the silence of an evening in Rome, seemed to show more reality than all the conjecture one has heard on the subject. These are the factors that should add up to a rational explanation. I am very well aware of this. But to explain beyond what I have done is difficult. It is difficult to communicate rationally the moving enigma of life.

CHAPTER III

Throne, Magna Charta, and Court

At first, the "hall of the throne" and the "pope's household" sound like simple matters, things one would read about in a diocesan newspaper. In reality, the pope's throne and household are the perfect background for certain observations on changes in the Vatican. To enter the papal apartments and to observe his private residence does not mean to dwell on the mere visual aspects of the profound changes taking place there. We are definitely at the "top" of the Vatican now, and at this level the meaning of everything is intensified. We find ourselves in a place where everything has clear symbolic value, and where the head and tail of the symbol, as it were, force us to universal considerations. It was here that many innovations were first exteriorized, so to speak. It will astound many to know that some of the most radical updatings took place here. For example, red, the ancient color of Roman Catholicism, the brilliant red of the damasks, or the dark red of the baldachins, the renowned "Catholic red" that has colored the history of the popes for centuries, has ceased in our day to be the color of the Vatican.

Entering into the pope's house we find nothing left of what the Vaticanologists found there only a few years ago. The second loggia, where even John XXIII ruled in the atmosphere of yesterday's world, has been stripped of its damasks, its black crucifixes, its semidarkness, its gilt chairs, its Chinese vases, its subdued lighting. We now find there a series of salons absolutely divested of the old "clerical" atmosphere and, against this new background, the Swiss guards and the papal gendarmes look like a surrealistic superimposition, a purely decorative leftover from vanished temporal power. With the ancient sumptuous damasks removed, the luxurious drapery taken down, the golden clocks in "archepiscopal" style eliminated, the revamping has been thorough.[1] We stroll through brightly lit halls opening into one another and leading to the throne and to the private library and these halls present to us an array of colors that smack of a modern household. The "cool" colors of today's taste for space predominate now, varying from light greens to icy blues and "champagne" yellows. Light is everywhere. And in the light, as in country villas, are the outlines of many plants. Primitive wooden sculpture, Della Robbias, and profane paintings of the *trecento* have taken the place of yellowed baroque oil paintings. In certain corners I found a refinement and elegance to match Berenson's home outside Florence. On the floor above, Paul VI has introduced teak into the furnishing of his private apartment. Everything leaves one with the impression of a violent rupture with the taste of yesterday. But even apart from the "functionalism" of the teak and considering only the official apartment itself, the change strikes one as immense. At times these cold colors, the magnificent pieces of antique furniture, the *prie-dieus* with little milk-colored cushions, all rigorously arranged in the modern geometry of "thicknesses," and the colors distributed with refinement, bring to mind the fashion of lay and worldly taste. Naturally certain criticism was raised against these renewals pushed through in the name of the polemic against Vatican "ostentation." But such criticism is really meaningless. Even John XXIII transformed a tower into a place where he could live, and took an innocent delight in luxury; it is said that he wanted the guards with the Turkish *colpak* (which Pius XII had eliminated) returned to the pontifical apartment.[2] Far more significant is the symbolism behind this radical transformation.

At the end of these halls now divested of the clerical look, we come to the new papal throne. The room is less spacious than the others, clear, absolutely without "red triumphalism" and with a play of turtledove grays instead, scantily enriched by an ancient sarcophagus in sculpted stone. Here we have the culminating expressions of the papacy's divestment of temporal power which we saw indicated in the papal apartment. We find here not another of yesterday's regal thrones in monarchic style and tied to temporal power. The baldachins and ostrich-plume fans (*flabelli*) are gone, and there are now only three steps and a seat of bare stone. The pope of Rome sits on this throne between two fourth-century sculptures found in the Vatican grottoes and originally belonging to the basilica of Constantine. The return to rock bottom, the departure from zero again, the desire springing from the council to return to pre-Constantinian Catholicism, and the renunciation of temporal power have reached here their maximum manifestation. There is that mixture of refinement and primitivism which one so often encounters in modern culture. One has the sensation of a cultivated and elegant Paleo-Christianity lived in an intellectual way.

As all visitors do, I stopped before this throne because it is the most discussed symbol of Paul VI's papacy. Here, in condensed form, are all the questions, all the suspicions, all the doubts that the "Pauline epoch" brings after the Johannine epoch. But we also find here many answers to those questions, doubts, and suspicions. The less gentle critics of Paul VI frequently speak of a renewal which goes no further than symbols. In the teak added to the private apartment of the pope and in his elegant Paleo-Christian throne they see the signs of an exclusively technocratic, intellectual, and aesthetic updating. I myself had an impression of aestheticism. But a consideration of the whole puts this impression into context. Besides the steps of bare stone, besides the symbolism, there now exists a different Vatican reality which takes its origin from this different throne. The throne represents the first real key for a serious consideration of Paul VI and the present Vatican. This throne goes far beyond the limits of a symbol. Perhaps it is we who should go beyond our suspicions of transformism and technocracy. For whatever can be said of any instrument of power can be said of this throne. It is a new and profoundly updated instrument. To be sure, it may be used in the future to make politics, and either progressive or conservative politics at that. However, there is no doubt that Paul VI and the council created here, and began here, the *aggiornamento* in depth.

I want to begin this discussion of the throne with a conversation I had with Bishop Carlo Colombo,[3] who is regarded today as Paul VI's confidential theologian and who is therefore, more than any other, the "man behind the throne." As a matter of fact, it would be difficult to think of any layman who could give a more "lay" orientation to things than this man gives. A prelate without purple ribbons, an intellectual of European stamp, reserved, incisive in his judgments, Colombo provided me with the key to the orientation one must give to the problem. An orientation, I should say, that would not displease a Hegelian. According to Colombo, only the historical approach can give us a real insight into the Vatican situation. Let me summarize briefly what this means. Perhaps it will bring us back to Paul VI's throne with clearer ideas.

The life of the Catholic Church, and hence of the Vatican, did not begin its "opening-up" process only in these council years. The process originated at the moment of the crisis of temporal power when the Church, after having walled itself in and closed itself off from the world, decided to begin a modest dialogue with the world. The first phase was the repeal of the famous *"non expedit"*—the papal order forbidding Catholics to participate in any way in the political life of Garibaldi's Italy. The second phase was the creation of Catholic Action and, with Pius XI, the initiation of a doctrinal statement on the situation of Christians in today's world, and the relaunching of the missionary program. The third phase, the exchanges with non-Catholics, was developed by Pius XII in countless allocutions. Finally the Church came to the phase where the gradual process reaching back to Pius X called for a decisive "leap forward" because the new course was straining under old regimes. And it fell to John XXIII to initiate the final move that brought on the council. He based his action upon six essential points. First, the Church is making the transition from a static phase to a phase of movement, a transition which must be understood, says Colombo, "as an effort to express the whole of reality." Second, the Church has decided upon a liturgical reform to express this new phase with a new form of worship. Third, the Church has decided to end the "apprehensive" way of looking at others and to make the transition to confidence by means of ecumenism. Fourth, the Church is making an effort to comprehend the real world even in its concrete forms, and to establish philosophically that the "concrete" is not alien to the religous sense of life. Fifth, a different evaluation of the real world means that religion is not limited to prayers and that the Church's "opening up" must therefore be extended to certain human themes such as peace, war, and the great social problems. And finally, given the transition to a new phase, the Church has decided to deal with the question of religious liberty, with all that this implies, such as concordats conceived as instruments not of privilege, but of agreement and collaboration; the separation of Church and state; the refusal to regard political power as an instrument for religious ends, etc. But all these essential points, Colombo says, presupposed a definition of the Church written into a document. And this exists today, formulated by the council in the famous constitution *De Ecclesia.*

For the first time in the history of the Church of Rome, there is alongside the pope's authority a Magna Charta which links the source of all authority and power to a definition of the nature of the Church and its mission. It is not a full and indissoluble link,[4] but it is solemn and binding since it represents the response of a council to the question, "What is the Church?" It is from this Magna Charta that derives the new vision of Roman Catholicism which has subjected even the relationship between papal primacy and the bishops to discussion, leading to the full affirmation of "collegiality" after centuries of indecision. But let us forget for the moment the institutional implications which we shall see later when we speak of collegiality and Vatican consultative-legislative power. Even considering simply the papal-Church relationship, this Magna Charta removes every hint of "adornment" from the throne I saw, and excludes the possibility of a reform reducible, for all its sweeping universality, to marginal modifications and affected rejuvenations. The constitution *De Ecclesia* is linked to the Johannine "conversion," to a Catholic Church that presents itself as a "recapitulation," as Guitton writes, "of all Christian experience, and repudiates the historical exclusiveness of 'Catholicism.'" Such concepts are not easy to understand. But it is significant that this Magna Charta was formulated in spite of the Church of Rome's having behind it thousands of years of dogmatic pronouncements, in spite of the complications and dictates of history, in spite of the habitual certainty that "everything has already been said." The popes who sit upon this throne in the future will find that a commitment has been made. The forms of that commitment are naturally vague: collegiality does not objectively modify the authority of the popes.[5] "But there is a logic of the Church," Bishop Colombo said, "which requires that many things be left vague, so that as time advances, things can adopt the form best suited to the times and the needs of the Church itself." And this sentence, spoken before the throne, struck me as perfect. The Vatican is going through a phase matched, in dramatic intensity, only by the Gregorian period or that of the Reformation. What is being reborn here has almost intangible forms because everything is being done with the long view. From the outside, we often see only the symbols and they strike us as shadows without bodies. But "there is a logic of the Church"—and the shadows are intentional. Such shadows can take concrete form in the future.

Naturally, many have been disappointed by this throne. They would have preferred a return to catacomb Christianity, a Ca-

tholicism without pomp, but also without sculpted stone. But
such criticism comes from a "simplicity cult" which takes issue
with luxury but which has its own form of demagogy.[6] While
I was visiting the papal household, I was told of the decision of
the council fathers to give their gold crosses to the poor, and of
the reversal of this decision when they realized that these "gold"
crosses were only gold-plated, and that they would have meant
only a modest and insignificant sum which would only be a disappointment to the poor destined to receive it. But if we
leave aside these controversies, which involve the individual
conscience more than the Catholic institution, the new pre-
Constantinian throne is profoundly significant. Elegant, and with
a distinct touch of the archaic, it is in any case the first reformed
throne of post-Vatican history. Reasoning as a layman, one can
draw a historical conclusion from this fact. This throne has a
constitution at its disposal, and it is enhanced by collegiality.
It is the property of an office which is infallible, but which is
also bound by ecumenism and by such principles as religous
liberty—which inevitably lead Catholicism to the relinquishment
of all temporal power and to new political ideologies. This throne,
therefore, symbolizes the end of a process which brought the
popes into conflict with history after dissolution of the medieval
theocracy. It declares the end of a millennium, that millennium
which in the spiral of reaction against political and temporal
decadence rendered the Church paradoxically more political and
temporal, pushing Catholicism to the heresies of Maurras and
to the definition of the Apostles as "twelve obscure Jews." The
popes destined to sit on this throne will have to lay aside their
Greco-Roman concept of history and reality, a concept so profoundly shaken by the modern struggle between Church and
state, and return to a more ancient one.

The word "throne" inevitably evokes the word "court." As a
matter of fact, many institutional reforms depend directly upon
how intense the Vatican court's interference is in the organs
of power. The old Vatican court is the source of continuous am-

biguities, being defended, fought, or condemned according to the interests of the hour. Troublesome phenomena such as those of Pius XII's reign are traceable to the old court, and certain long-since-irrelevant Vatican formalisms stand firmly rooted in it. It is not pleasant to see an incomparable household, full of artistic treasure and authentic sacredness, overrun by various anachronistic phenomena in the style of the principality of Monaco for the sole pleasure of indulging whoever happens to be administering this court. To hear it said that Roman nobility and soldiers with headpieces à la Buckingham Palace are necessary to protract in time the Renaissance splendor of the Church, makes one wonder about the fame the Renaissance is enjoying here. The truly regal Vatican is the non-touristic Vatican, with its rooms inhabited by priests and cardinals living an extremely busy and unostentatious life there. But neither should we be overcritical of a court which deserves a frank yet demythologizing analysis. Naturally, my observations may not be shared by everyone. Everyone defends a Vatican that suits his own taste, and none of us like to depart from habit. If we speak of the Vatican in simple and even raw terms so as not to falsify a reality which adulation and the "respect complex" have deformed almost as much as the satire of its opponents, we will only provoke criticism. Still, I believe that an optic truth has its advantages in conveying certain impressions of the so-called "secret Vatican" which rotates about the throne.

The world that moves about a pope is too mobile a reality today to permit irrevocable statements. But when I think back to the days I passed in the area of the second loggia, I recall only a series of experiences that contribute to the demystification of many commonplaces. Much is said, in fact, of a closed and isolated Vatican; of bishops and cardinals walled up in ancient positions of luxury and autocracy; of a "court" that conditions and hinders the pope from having modern human relationships. They even speak of the pope himself as perpetuating the institution and ways of an absolute sovereign. There is no doubt an element of truth in many such statements. But, at the same time, Vatican life seems to be so different and so rich in new perspectives, and so much less ritualistic than is thought, that we find we have to regard most of such criticism as based on incomplete information.

Every pope naturally has his "style," and this can often be deceiving. But if we take Paul VI's style as a starting point, we may be able to reach some kind of conclusion. Paul VI has certainly contributed to certain changes. The disappearance of the *flabelli* and the baldachin during processions, the enunciation of the tiara, and the very style of the pope's way of living, all tend to create a different atmosphere in the Vatican. One should not cite as fact that which is difficult to verify, but Paul VI does seem to be an intellectual decidedly bent upon contact with life and ideas. His very figure moves in the grandness of these places freighted with history, withdrawing even from the outward signs of a "court" and especially from "courtier" entanglements. This is revealed, superficially perhaps, in his manner of dress, his work habits, his taste and choice of friends. Paul VI wears a white habit reduced to the very essentials of symbolism. He refused the famous pontifical slippers ("Something for opera singers," he called them in the first days of his reign) and he has adopted a simplified plan of living. Taking issue with his "pauperism," some criticize sharply certain of his decisions such as the construction of a terrace on top of the Apostolic Palace or the renovation of the papal apartments. But, here again, it is a question of purely polemic criticism. We have already noted that Paul VI introduced a modification of "clerical" ostentation, taking from the Vatican storage rooms works of art valued by modern culture and following the Berensonian trend. We might add that he does not live in a household modeled after the schemes of a princely establishment of the Renaissance, but in a house that takes its dignity from culture and intelligence. Paul VI often invites guests and friends to his table. And the terrace he had built meant a refusal of the stroll as a "rite." The repose of the pope no longer means the arranging of the guard, orders, counterorders, and a corps of escorts for the traditional daily walk in the Vatican gardens. Paul VI works until dinner at nine o'clock in the evening. After dinner he goes out onto the terrace above his rooms. He requires only an internal stairway and the company of his secretaries. The pope sees the lights of Rome, says the rosary, and goes back downstairs to resume his work. There is less and less "court" life. The "man dressed in white" lives a logic of power like an absolute sovereign. But as this logic assimilates certain changes (and we have seen how), the absolute-monarchy aspect of the Vatican is losing many of its outward characteristics. The pope lives in the Vatican, to put it in rough terms, as the President of the United States lives in the White House. He has less of the joys of the profane life, and more of the solitude of his mission.

Paul VI has made of the Vatican an obviously new world. Behind him is the shadow of the man who perhaps counted most in the pope's life, that of Father Bevilacqua,[7] the "parish-priest cardinal." The pastoral values and intellectual values which had met in such complete synthesis in the parish-priest cardinal come through in the "style" of a pope who reads both St. Augustine and Maritain. Paul VI is a pope who elevated to the archbishopric of Turin an "Augustinian" professor, Monsignor Michele Pellegrino, who in the council deplored the existence of a "Catholic pragmatism" which over-esteems the "outward works of the apostolate" and neglects interior and intellectual life. Father Bevilacqua was bitterly opposed to Vatican ostentation, and he even criticized the custom of the military escort of cardinals "because even housemaids go with the *carabinieri*" (Italian armed police). And Paul VI is as far from "pragmatism" as he is from this cult of formality. He is surrounded by men who cultivate only certain values, such as the theologian Bishop Carlo Colombo and a secretary who studies Bernanos and the problem of evil. His ties to scholarly laymen like Guitton are well known. But neither is it a question of a crew of eggheads. It is a matter of a human background traceable to the figure of Father Bevilacqua and to Montinian liberal Catholicism. One often notes in the Vatican the North Italian atmosphere of the "parish-priest cardinal," in a mixture of intellectual and pastoral life. The sensation

I had is that the Vatican is going through a period of transition
even in this sense. Much is said of Paul VI as a pope who is undecided about liquidating the "court" and who is hesitating between the demobilization of the Roman aristocracy and a political
program incapable of drastic provisions. But if I had to judge, I
would say that the problem is not seen correctly. In reality there
are two "courts" around the pope; one is a "technical court"
made up of counselors, cardinals, and the apparatus of the secretariat, and this is the court which really counts. Then, alongside this, there still lives, without any influence in Vatican life
whatsoever, what remains of the old court. They are two adjacent
worlds which no longer communicate with one another. The
second is decidedly in decline. Daily life in the Vatican struck
me rather as the mirror of a nonexistent "court" that is revived
only for certain ceremonies.

This reviving of the old court is certainly open to criticism.
But frankly it seems to be more a "conditioned reflex" of tradition
than a "presence" of tradition itself. In the Church's politics in
the strict sense, only the official counselors of the secretariat and
of the Curia really count. Only the opinions of the intellectuals
and theologians surrounding the pope really come to bear on decisions. But the traditional court, that which swells the *Annuario
pontificio* to make it look like a dictionary, is gradually becoming a pure name. Behind the Swiss guards, during the day there
is only the world of the bureaucracy, the Secretariat of State, and
the Curia. One cannot speak of a "court," because everything is
reduced to essentials and the court is limited to the usual two
gendarmes and the usual ushers who stand out only because they
are robed in red and are called *sediari*.[8] Then in the evening the
Vatican is truly deserted. The cardinals retire into their apartments where they live with widowed sisters and are assisted by
a few nuns. The pope closes himself up in his few rooms to read
or converse with the two priests that have been living with him
for years and whom he calls informally "Don Bruno" and "Don
Pasquale." Then one understands that the household Vatican,
the fortress Vatican, and the labyrinth Vatican are really nothing

more than a "big parish house" which epitomizes the lonelinesses and customs of parish houses all over the world. The only difference is that here live powerful men who dedicate their life to religious power. Some may feel that to demystify the Vatican in this way means to desecrate it, or to defend or to make use of an irreverent perspective. But I do not believe that the Church asks to be loved as a myth. Neither do I believe that taking a more simple view means either to defend or desecrate anything. A new Vatican, a more gray and more genuine Vatican, does exist. And this is the background against which the present transitions in the Church can be put into their true perspective.

The day may come when this pope will modify such an atmosphere, or when later popes will modify it after him. But there is no doubt that the problem of post-Vatican Catholicism does not lie in the court. The problem now, so far as consultative and deliberative power is concerned, is found in the relationship between the pope and the synod of bishops. Or, in questions of executive power, between the pope and the Curia. The obstacle to many renovations can come from imperious men of the old school and of an administrative mentality who not infrequently run the Curia in able resistance to the pope. But the collegial throne of today appears stronger, even in this connection, than the solitary throne of yesterday. Let us go on now to see what the Magna Charta means in placing, for the first time in history, a small parliament of bishops next to the throne. The visit to the pope's house does not end here. Certain transformations are so little symbolic that they require a special analysis of the power which has been released from the throne. So now let us see how collegiality renews the Vatican's top level of power.

CHAPTER IV

Bishops, Cardinals, and Power: Colombo

One morning I saw workmen in the courtyard of St. Damasus. They were making ready the hall where the episcopal synod was to meet to assist Paul VI in the government of the Church of Rome. The meeting was the first time in history that bishops were to enter the Vatican to share in the power of the pope. To see a meeting place being built there, even though it was not really parliamentary in significance, makes a definite impression on modern sensibilities. In the Vatican palaces there will now be two halls dedicated to consultative assemblies. On the third floor, there is the Hall of the Consistory, where the cardinals, who form the executive body of the Church, elect the pope. On the ground floor is now the Hall of the Synod for the bishops who will form a sort of Roman consultative body. It is not a question of two houses, one "upper" and the other "lower." It would be inexact to speak of bicameralism or of the liberal evolution of power, even though these reforms in the very heart of papal power look like the arrival—in diversified and attenuated form—of a sort of democracy in Vatican absolute monarchism. It would be an exaggeration to say that the rigid area of absolutism and infallibility has been conditioned or changed in any way.

It is only that we now note within that area a different relationship between freedom and authority.

Bishops in the Vatican: There is no doubt that this image provokes an idea of rupture, a breach in the walls of the last absolute monarch, the idea of the insinuation of a collegial power in the pontifical world. Nor can it be denied that the problem arose in the council, out of the clash between the bishops and the Curia and the battle against authoritarian and arbitrary Romanism. But the logic of the Church has found a solution to the conflict in the terms "renewal" and "continuity." In investigating this subject, one has the sensation of touching on the key to the laws that govern a closed and theocratic society. Anyone who studies the problem of power finds himself, as it were, in the underground darkness of forces which, like springs, perpetuate themselves without changing. And it is here that we see how possible it is for the Vatican to change while the Church itself remains unchanged. It is here that the image comes of a ray of light hitting on a surface of water and, as the point of impact shifts, the light illuminates the bottom differently, changing its shadows, its projections, its relationships, but never changing the bottom itself. And again I found this image fitting the self-regenerating power of the Vatican. The papal throne and collegiality are subtle relationships exposed today to an "impact of light" that varies them without crystallizing them into fixed forms. The following account of a conversation with the Archbishop of Milan brings out the point of this problem.

Cardinal Giovanni Colombo, the Archbishop of Milan, is certainly the most authoritative Italian leader of the episcopal forces that come to the Vatican today with these new consultative and exceptionally deliberative powers.[1] He comes from the educational field, from the university world of the seminaries, and he is at the head of a large and important diocese. He has just become one of the "troika" that presides over the Italian episcopal conference and, as such (to use somewhat improper but clear language), he is therefore the top and bottom man. In a schoolroom that looks out on the cupola of St. Peter's, I had an opportunity one day to speak with him about all these institutional innovations. I found his words to be a veritable X ray of the "power forces" that are in the process of regenerating themselves. This robust and kindly cardinal, an ex-rector of seminaries and a bishop capable of epitomizing both the "basic forces" of the clergy and those of the religious intelligentsia, spent a long Roman afternoon helping me to come to grips with the true drift of certain historical events that are taking place in the Vatican. And that talk struck me as a perfect documentation of the conciliar and post-conciliar Vatican.

Cardinal Colombo told me that "to understand these problems we must begin from the concept of authority. The authority of the Church expresses itself in two forms, the one being expressed personally through the pope, and the other collegially through the episcopate. We are dealing here with simultaneous authority because while the pope 'personally' governs the entire Church, the episcopal college in its turn collegially governs the entire Church—for episcopal authority has two dimensions, expressed either in one diocese or in a plurality of dioceses. Hence it cannot be said that authority finds new collegial forms, since those forms already exist. The Synod of Bishops, for example, was suggested and solicited by the concept of the collegiality of the episcopate as authoritatively promulgated by Vatican II in the constitution *Lumen Gentium.* As a matter of fact, that constitution made possible a vivid awareness that the Church is not only founded upon the "rock" of the pope, the successor of Peter, but also upon the entire episcopal body or college as successor to the college of the Apostles. This heightened awareness is destined to produce in the future specific and concrete forms for a distinct articulation and distribution of power between pope and bishops. In the Synod of Bishops one can already see one of these forms. And still, the synod is not to be absolutely identified or confused with episcopal collegiality, or with the ecumenical council which is collegiality's highest expression."

With the calm of a university professor, the archbishop proceeded to make distinctions. "The episcopal college," he said, "cannot be conceived without its head, the Roman pontiff, as it exercises a supreme and full power over the whole Church through the will of Christ. Christ himself wanted the bishops to succeed the Apostles 'as shepherds of the Church,' and the authority which they possess comes to each bishop directly from Christ, although—as is obvious—no one can exercise it except in hierarchical communion with the head and with the other members of the college. For this reason, the episcopal college, being a divine institution, is perfect and stable in the Church and it cannot be suppressed by any authority, not even by that of the pope. In the same way, there exists an episcopal power that expresses itself in the council with full collegiality. Since it is in the ecumenical council that the bishops exercise in a solemn way their supreme authority over the entire Church, it follows that whatever they affirm and establish in ecumenical council, even though it requires the confirmation of the pope, is affirmed and established in virtue of the inherent and proper authority that they receive directly from Christ, and not by virtue of a delegation they may receive from the pope. In ecumenical council the bishops are not delegates of the pope, and neither is the power they exercise there delegated."

Cardinal Colombo then went on to explain that "thus, by institution of the very founder of the Church, the supreme authority has two expressions, the one personal in the pope, and the other collective in the episcopal college. Compared to the episcopal college, however, the nature and power of the Synod of Bishops is quite different. The Synod of Bishops was established by Paul VI and is a papal, not a divine, institution. Indeed, it is subject to change or even to suppression. It is a human institution, and hence transitory. It was occasioned by the fact that episcopal collegiality became better known and taught through Vatican II, but it exhausts neither the depth nor the universality of the collegial power of the episcopate. The Synod of Bishops is an organ with a permanent character, but it enters into operation only when the pope convokes it to deal with a particular matter. The college of bishops, on the other hand, is always functioning, even though it is not always united in council. Furthermore, most of the members of the synod have their jurisdiction only for the study and solution of a specific problem, while membership in the episcopal college derives from the bishop's consecration and does not cease so long as his hierarchical communion with the head and members of the college continues. The Synod of Bishops is therefore a consultative organ (and only sometimes deliberative, only by direct delegation of specific deliberative power from the pope) of the personal government of the pope, and it is destined to play a role of great significance and importance with the pope and among the bishops."

Then, concluding, Cardinal Colombo said: "The synod will bring the pope a living and immediate experience of the problems and needs of his flock. The bishops who will compose it will come for the most part from the pastoral work of the Church. The pope cannot enjoy personally, in such a measure, the same constructive and salutary immersion in practical experience; nor can the members of his Curia, who also lack direct contact with the vastness and multiplicity of the conflicts, the anxieties, and the problems of concrete Christian life. In meeting with these bishops, the pope will be able better to feel the pulse of the Church and the world, able better to listen to their concerns, and able better to propose remedies with more delicate and attentive efficacy. The synod will furthermore provide the pope with the opportunity to know personally many bishops recognized as being of great worth and energy by the same authorities that will send them to the synod, and to choose among them to obtain valuable collaborators whenever the need arise. The bishops of the synod are for the most part to be nominated directly by individual episcopal conferences; and they are to be nominated specially every time, on the basis of their specific competence in connection with the particular problem for which the synod is convoked on that occasion. This will circumvent that sclerosis of old age which so often paralyzes organisms and institutions whose members are elected for life or for a long period.

Then, for the bishops, the synod will be—each time it convenes —a clear call to feel more vividly that responsibility for the whole Church which they share collegially with the pope, and it will provide them with a concrete way of acting on their concern and solicitude for the universal Church."

Let us stop here. Begun before the pope's throne and terminated with this conversation, I think the "problem of power" has become a bit clearer now. From the institutional viewpoint, this episcopal synod really constitutes an elaboration of the pope's *personal* government; it would be inexact to speak of it as "neoliberalism in the Vatican" because this would imply the idea of democracy as necessary to the very nature of authority. But there is no doubt that, even with "Romanism" and infallibility remaining intact, the entrance of the world's bishops into the administration of Roman power signifies a revolutionary departure. With the laws that govern a theocratic society unaltered from the dogmatic point of view, the Vatican is beginning to make use of efficient organs capable of expressing individual opinions and bringing about a sort of "aristocratic" democracy. In a constitutional structure which includes the twofold principle of personal authority and collegiality, a way has been found for expressing institutionally a "plurality" of instruments which is indispensable in modern times. The pope can—but is not required to—have recourse to the bishops for major decisions, and so we cannot say that authority has been modified; but the bishops represent a new consultative, and at times even deliberative, power. The synod exists, even if it depends upon the pope to use it with more or less frequency. The phase that is now about to begin is difficult to describe. But here again a theologian clarified things for me. The Vatican can in the future place its accent on the collegial aspect or upon the personal aspect of power, according to the circumstances and needs and objectives pursued. The pope, this symbol of unity, is like a joint between unity and the multiplicity symbolized by the bishops. But, as a joint, he can sense the thrusts and counterthrusts of influence and power, and in mediating between various forces the Vatican can face the post-conciliar age equipped with the diverse instruments and consequent elasticity it needs in a pluralistic world. These distinctions are always subtle and perhaps never really comprehensible. But in dealing with this whole question we find ourselves, as I said before, on the very point of "impact" between the ancient light of the Church and the surface of the new reality. We find ourselves at the very center of the refractions as they change, in the midst of the confusion of projections as they emerge. The impact has hardly begun to make itself felt, and we are taken by surprise much as if we were in the middle of a "plankton culture" full of germinations.

The cardinals are also involved in the problem of top-level power. We can deal with them here, now that the reader has been introduced to the whole problem. For with the entrance of the bishops into the "chamber of buttons," the position of the cardinals is definitely questionable. Only yesterday they represented the elite at the top of an elective monarchy, something like the "ten" in the ancient Republic of Venice. But the institutional problem of the sacred college of cardinals has been very precisely stated by many theologians. Hans Küng, the liberal German theologian called by John XXIII to the council as a *peritus* or expert, has written that one of the tasks of the new Catholic age is a reassessment of the role of the sacred college. According to Küng, one of the decisions that we should expect in the future "is the transferring of the elections of the pope from the sacred college of cardinals to the counsel of bishops that is finally emerging as the true representative organ of the Church."[2] It is not my purpose here to say whether or not it would be good if this did take place. To be sure, the role of the cardinals is a complicated matter. It is difficult to speak of the cardinalate in terms of decline, and the shadings and nuances of the problem are infinite. I trust that the reader will bear with me if I limit myself merely to describing the over-all situation rather than relating a long series of details.

The cardinals are not, as the bishops are, an "order" deriving authority—according to the Church—from the Apostles. The cardinal's dignity became important only for historical reasons around the year 1000, when, in order to take the election of the pope out of the power of the emperor and the nobility, the sacred college of cardinals was given the role of choosing the pope and of guarding papal authority in those periods when there is no pope to exercise it. But the cardinals, as a college, are never the "subjects" of authority, not even when there is no pope. They are and remain at all times only its "keepers." Not even when they elect the pope do they confer authority; they only choose the person in whom authority will be vested. This distinction is important for establishing the fact that the cardinals as such are never the sources of authority in the sense that the bishops are. And it is from this distinction that all the complications arise. This is better understood when one recalls that it was with a view to solving this problem that John XXIII decided to name all the cardinals to episcopal rank. But this did not obtain the brilliant results he expected, for not all cardinals can enter into the synod, and many bishops that take part in it do not have the rank of cardinal. The cardinals may each have an episcopal authority; but they do not therefore constitute, when united in sacred college, anything new in spite of John XXIII's "cleaning out." They remain "dignitaries" who guard the papal authority when the pope dies and who exercise the highest prerogative in electing the new pope. As far as the problem of authority is concerned, the cardinals' position as a college remains what it always was.

But let us consider the power from another point of view. The sacred college of cardinals may also be regarded as an assembly performing consultative functions at the pope's side. As a result of the advance of history, however, it is at best only an atrophied consultative body. The sacred college exercised such functions in the past. Even Pius XI seems to have sought the opinions of the cardinals gathered in consistory; however, the consistory is now a "silent senate" with no consultative or deliberative role in the government of the Church. As a "body" or college, the cardinals have no weight in this area. Individually, however, they do have

enormous power in the executive branch of Church government. As a matter of fact, the cardinals are, by right, members
of all the congregations of the Curia—that is, of all the ministries or departments of the executive branch. And they are
usually heads or members of a number of congregations. Thus,
they advise the pope as individuals, and even help him to decide on a matter; but, even within the framework of the executive branch, it is impossible to speak of their participation as a
body in the power of the Church. Furthermore, many cardinals
who are members of ministries live in remote parts of the world,
and only the cardinals of the Roman Curia residing in Rome form
the true executive branch. It is this that gives rise to the famous
evil of "Romanism." But we will speak of this later on when we
take up the question of the Curia.

What we have said about the cardinals clearly brings us to
the most difficult part of our examination of Catholic institutions
and power. Considered in its three roles (as guardian of the authority in the election of the pope, "silent senate" as a consultative assembly, and controlling element in the Roman executive
organs) the sacred college is a veritable Gordian knot. We cannot speak of a decline in the cardinalate, because the "dignity"
is definitely laden with superpower, and has a practical monopoly both of executive and elective power. It may be said, however, that with the creation of the Synod of Bishops, the sacred
college is no longer the only representative assembly attached
to the papal throne. The council has relaunched the authority of
the bishops and it is possible that a historical process has been
set in motion that is destined to modify the elective monarchy
functioning à la Republic of Venice. But predictions of the outcome are impossible. For alongside the victory of the bishops,
there has been, as a matter of fact, a relaunching of the college
of cardinals. With the latest consistories, the sacred college has
grown significantly to include several patriarchs and to constitute
a supernational representation which has profoundly "de-Roman-
ized" it. It can be said that no state possesses such a diversified
and authoritative "senate," a senate capable of uniting the most

multifarious representatives of the European, Asiatic, African, and American worlds. But even though reconstituted, we are still dealing here with a "silent" senate. What will become of it still remains unclear. And I frankly have not even succeeded in seeing what general trends are in view. On the contrary, I had the impression that many areas of the new Vatican, the Vatican in formation, are destined to become irretrievably entangled by the decision to renovate without changing. The cardinals remain an open problem, another blank page of the future. And such blank pages are as incomprehensible as the tangles that could arise. There is more than a little of the Byzantine in these problems of the upper levels.[3]

I visited the consistory hall on the second loggia where the cardinals meet. And there I had a vivid impression of how little balance there is between the various aspects of the Catholic renewal. The most ancient senate of the world continues to meet in this hall. The council is bringing its weight to bear and new instruments are being born, but the old instruments are not being given new forms. Everything overlaps; everything is interwoven. And this helps us to account for the "gradualism" in Paul VI's decisions. Still we have no trouble in seeing why this "Pauline gradualism" (or the "Johannine thrust," for that matter) cannot really produce many results. A rusting in the Roman institutional machinery corrodes the circumspect and prudent decisions of Paul VI as much as it did the brilliant and improvised solutions of John XXIII. The future will tell which knots will be untied and which will be pulled even tighter in an institution that escapes the understanding of man. But at least I have put the question as clearly as I am able.

I have only one memory of the sacred college, and it is of a February morning during the consistory of 1965. Cardinals and patriarchs in silks, jewels, and gold entered with their shortened, but still very lengthy, trains. On the grandstands of St. Peter's, standing seminarians and parish priests were applauding. I remember a country priest from North Italy, in torn shoes, clapping his hands and at the same time growling: "And *this* is the

74

Church that's cutting down on ostentation and returning to the Apostles and to Jesus." The applause was wild and moving; but the dissatisfaction was just as moving and interminable. Such are the contradictions of today's Catholicism with its capacity for simultaneously loving and criticizing institutions. Certain atrophies of power and certain forms of hierarchy are no doubt being subjected to a critical strain which tends to dissolve and clarify the anomalies of the transition. The cardinals are loved as bishops, but as hierarchs they always find in the things left unexpressed a way of escaping criticisms. If I were to attempt to draw any conclusions here, I would deceive my readers. The transition is evident to all, but the renewal is difficult.

CHAPTER V

The Secretariat of State: Cicognani

I spent many days in the Secretariat of State. To reach it, one passes through the big bronze door, up the same stairway that leads to the apartment of the pope, and finally one finds oneself in the courtyard of St. Damasus surrounded by pontifical gendarmes and Swiss guards. The atmosphere is the same that prevails in the courtyards of the papal household, except that here it is perhaps a bit more disciplined. When a cardinal appears, a simple clap of the hands is enough to make chauffeurs jump to. Dry orders and soldiers' salutes generate a more "military" than clerical atmosphere. And it is a constant reminder of the fact that Catholicism is a form of "warfare." Then two ancient elevators take one to the third loggia. The third loggia's windows open onto St. Peter's Square and overlook all of Rome. It is the "decision center" of the Vatican world.

The Secretariat of State is of necessity the first stop for anyone who wants to observe the world of the "apparatus." It is in fact here that that labyrinth of red damask offices comprised in the Curia opens up. And it is here that begins that complex of powers dominated by bishops and cardinals, that executive structure often described as monolithic and inaccessible to the

77

"council winds." Here is the entrance into the mysterious realm of ancient customs, of a bureaucracy without secrets, and of the so-called unchangeable techniques of government. Strictly speaking, the Secretariat of State is not the Curia; that is, it is not the world of the Church government, ministries, or departments. It is a sort of "little Curia," a duplicate of the Curia itself or a summary of the Curia in the form of a "pope's cabinet." The Secretary of State is at once a vice-pope, a premier, a foreign minister, and a superintendent of the pontifical cabinet. The Secretariat of State is a filter through which all decisions pass to be translated into lines of religious policy and politics in the true and strict sense of the word. But it is the top, and the epitome, of the Curia—even physically. The pope receives visitors and works on the third floor. The Secretary of State lives on the second. The Secretariat of State is on the fourth floor. From this point the whole political and bureaucratic apparatus of the Curia unfolds—and it easily suggests the idea of an "ivory tower." This world is frequently contrasted with that of the council because these offices, where concordats, diplomatic policies, and administrative decisions are worked out, represent a Constantinianism—a political, imperial Church—that the council either rejected or discussed extensively.

The Secretariat of State may definitely be the point of friction between the reforming intentions of a pope and the Vatican administrative mentality. One can find there today enthusiastically "conciliar" men of the young generation, and its future is anything but guaranteed. I am personally convinced that the change of generations will either disrupt the routine or radically change the criteria of action. I definitely found many intelligent and open-minded functionaries there, including even a number of young "Johannine" diplomats. But the fact remains that tradition has established the Secretariat of State as the "home stretch" in the ecclesiastical career of imperious and "administrative" men, and a great number of adherents to the "old regime" are definitely well entrenched there.

Some of the offices of the Secretariat are bare and painted in flat white, while others are still, after two pontificates, tapestried with the symbols of Pius XII, and the contrast is a perfect illustration of the polemic going on in the Vatican. Not that this polemic is necessarily conscious and intentional in all its manifestations. For side by side with the group of Pacellians still tenaciously holding the key positions and following old diplomatic lines, there are the new men who are quick, decisive, and dynamic technicians. Obviously, a transfer of power is being prepared. Many new "teams" could definitely be formed out of the very men who had key roles in organizing the council, men who proved not only their outstanding capacities for governing but also an ability to resist the most revoutionary theses when they judged it necessary. These neo-technocrats remind one of ancient pontifical legates. I am not saying that they are capable of blocking the initiative of the pope, but it can be observed that a readoption of not strictly "conciliar" ways of dealing with problems is always possible. It is furthermore probable that Paul VI will show himself to be a decidedly post-Johannine pope when he gets down to resolving the problem of the Secretariat of State. Paul VI is isolated and comparatively new, and he finds himself surrounded by many dignitaries who stand and watch, without taking a position. As long as Secretary of State Cicognani is alive, however, there will be no major crisis in the Secretariat of State. This sector of Vatican life definitely feels the beneficial influence of the sincere and kindly octogenarian who heads it. It is clearly due for a restructuring, however, and the careful observer already detects new reflexes in the lines of the Secretariat of State. I will mention here only a few that strike me as significant.

On the ground floor of this world I paid a visit to the Secretary of State, Amleto Cardinal Cicognani.[1] It was a sunny morning. The sunlight entered into the red salon of the antechamber and shone on the gilt consoles and seemed to intensify an ambassadorial and palatial atmosphere that history has left here more than elsewhere in the Vatican. There was a time when the Secretary of State controlled the entire temporal power of the

Papal States, commanded the prefects, the police, the army. Subsequently he became a premier and a foreign minister, an alter ego and first counselor to the pope. On his shoulders now rest the responsibilities of a different form of temporal power. Under him are the Secretary for Extraordinary Affairs and the Substitute for Ordinary Affairs. He is therefore in charge of relations between the Church and states, concordat politics, diplomacy, direction of Secretariat personnel, Catholic Action, control of Vatican finances, etc. On the desk of the Secretary of State, at which such figures as Rampolla and Gasparri have sat, form is given to the political lines of a pontificate and to the policies that bind and shape a pontificate. The Secretary's role is, in fact, to act as chief of staff to the pope, and he generally resigns and leaves on the death of the pontiff who appointed him. But this is not the case with Cicognani, who had been appointed by John XXIII and was retained by Paul VI, obviously to underline the continuity present in the most political sector of Vatican government.

Cardinal Cicognani came toward me all smiles and joviality. He is a short, corpulent, and likably sanguine man of obvious northern Italian origin. He never for a moment shows his eighty-two years. His study is dominated by a large table of French design, a superb crucifix, and tapestries in shades of gold. Against this background, he moves with an affable and congenial frankness. Having been apostolic delegate to the United States throughout the entire pontificate of Pius XII, his North Italian expressions are interspersed with interesting Americanisms. "Yes, yes," he said as he sat down, "we are actually at a *turning point.*" Then, looking out through his thick glasses with a bright smile, he turned his attention to the technical reform that is destined to reach deeply into the Secretariat of State. "To build the Church," he said, "means to build an edifice that is never to be finished. It's like what the Milanese call a work that is always *in progress:* building the cathedral. The fact is, every age has its methods and its techniques. We are now in the process of bringing the Vatican organization *up to date.* It is definitely wrong to speak of 'reformation'; that term is really overworked these days. What term should we use? I don't know. Perhaps we should speak of a technical revision of the whole organization in line with the needs of today's world."

On delicate questions, the Secretary of State tended to become a bit elusive. For example, when I asked about the politics of Paul VI's pontificate, he said: "What are the political lines of this pontificate? To be honest, I don't believe this pope is making politics. He is working for peace and religion." He let me go on about Paul VI's "disengagement policy" being a consequence of the relinquishment of temporal power that seems to characterize this pontificate more and more; but then he stopped me with a wave of his hand. "Those are terms used outside, not here. They don't really apply here. I wouldn't even know how to comment on them." But then his naturally open temperament, a temperament ripened through years of experience in America, overcame his diplomatic reticence. "In any case," he said, "many new things are happening. This is the hour of renewal in all quarters. At times it is hard to understand it. As always, the new appears as imperfect, and the situation is delicate. But there is no doubt that great and new things are under way."

Once in this terrain, the cardinal proceeded with his guard down. And when he had finished, he took up a subject of my suggestion and developed it with pleasure. It was the question of Church-state relations in the light of the new principles laid down by the council. "The work of the council has a great bearing upon Church-state relations. Take religious liberty, for example. It is an important principle, and we should know exactly what it means in this area. It has been made out to be so complicated, you know. But if we reduce it to simple terms, there aren't any complications. It's a question of establishing the fact that the state must allow religious liberty for everyone. It is not a principle that subjects the truth of the Catholic religion to discussion; it is only a principle which asserts the dignity of man and which is derived from human dignity. Obviously, then, it is important to make it a rule for everybody—both for states and for Churches.

We don't have to hesitate for fear that it will contradict our Catholic convictions. We have no doubt about being the repositories of the true faith. Our truth is our most precious possession, and we will always defend it. But we don't deny that truth when we say that man has a right to religious freedom. Naturally it is in everyone's interest that the state give religious freedom to all, and that they establish the limits dictated by propriety and mutual respect. If the Mohammedans want to preach in Rome, they should be free to do so. But if they want to erect a mosque in St. Peter's Square, they should be dissuaded from doing so. The limits imposed by propriety should be judged according to the situation in each particular case. The freedom of other religions should not be a limitation on our freedom. In any case it is good that this affirmation of the dignity of man be clearly asserted."

All the while he was speaking, the cardinal was smiling. And he was obviously pursuing the conversation with his American pragmatism. At one point, he spoke of Milan as a "modern, alive city" which he evidently likes immensely. As I was taking leave of him, he went to meet Cardinal Spellman who had just arrived for a visit. These two grand old men represent the mentality of the "new world," a world that is certainly not that of the Curia; and they met each other with obvious mutual pleasure. And this coincidental scene put the finishing touch on the world of the Secretariat: Cicognani sustaining the thesis of religious freedom with the language and force that the American bishops showed in the council. This was anything but a sign of "Roman triumphalism" fossilized at the top level of power.

One could interpret this brief conversation with the Secretary of State in a number of ways. The fact that the new doctrinal positions are sustained with such force in the very heart of the "political" executive branch leads one to believe that new ways of understanding concordat politics have already been established. But rather than make premature judgments, perhaps we should limit ourselves to an observation. To find such un-Constantinian positions right in the "ivory tower" is an indication of how strong the phenomenon of self-regeneration is at every level of Catholicism, and how active it is in all the areas of the system. It is clearly an error to give a "vertical" interpretation to the process that is going on, an interpretation which represents the base as moving and renewing itself and the top as resisting the "renewal from below," or at best only letting itself be dragged forward. What is actually happening is something quite different. Innovations and transformations are coming both from below and from above. They flow from the council and from the pope who is of course advised by his own governmental apparatus. The difference is that when they come from the pope, they emerge wrapped up in technical difficulties. The "little Curia" too is strongly conscious of the Church's revolutionary renunciation of temporal power and its turning from merely diplomatic and administrative interests to other concerns. But this consciousness is inevitably conditioned by practical exigencies here. There is the necessity of administering current affairs, making treaties, and conducting diplomatic activities; even though the principles are changed, these remain the inherent task of the Vatican administrative structure. A theologian may find it easy to justify certain transformations on doctrinal grounds. Indeed it is common practice for lawmakers to leave constitutional innovations vague so that they can be given different forms in the centuries that follow. But for the bureaucracy, the jump between two epochs must be reduced to a day-to-day procedure. It registers clashes, divisions, and contradictions, and it must temper and resolve them into smooth practical operation. What looks like immobility is perhaps only the slowness of effecting an integration between the old and the new, and the "ideological position" of the man at the top may play a large role here. It is hardly mere chance that a Secretary of State selects religious freedom for a topic of conversation and develops it with so much spontaneity, revealing anti-Curial positions in the nucleus of the Curia itself. Still, behind this ideological position are the objective obstacles of a bureaucracy which in any case needs a change of generations and a technical reform. The Secretariat is regarding this reform in terms of a "restructuring." The world that opens up beyond the office of the Secretariat of State is in fact full of historical veneers, superimposed manners, and responsibilities tangled up by years of inertia. Pius XII brought to the Secretariat his centralizing mentality, abolishing the office of Secretary of State and replacing it with a principle. "The pope needs executors, not collaborators." With no Secretary existing in the Pacellian period, there were two almost contrasting worlds within the Secretariat, two lines called at that time the "Montini" and the "Tardini" lines. The result was a sort of political bivalence obtained by means of a Substitute Secretary of anti-Fascist, and liberal Catholic stamp (Montini), and a more available Secretary for Extraordinary Affairs (Tardini). This double posture obviously produced complications, overlappings, and even organizational divisions. Relations with Italy, for example, which should have been the business of the diplomatic section, were also maintained by the section of the Substitute Secretary. Even those in charge admitted that "the papers waltz from one section to the other because frequently not even the Secretaries are able to decide who is responsible." The ordinary affairs are no longer merely "internal" affairs, and neither are extraordinary affairs merely "external" affairs. The Secretariat is a structural muddle which two pontificates have left for Paul VI to straighten out. The projects of reform are aimed at making it into a chancery set up along clear lines.

Although there is a problem of "restructuring" and of "turnover," there is clearly no problem of a ruling class and a staff. The world of the Secretariat of State moves behind the historical veneers and the tangles of authority with incredible agility. The Secretariat is of workshop dimensions and it is nevertheless unbelievably efficient, even without electronic office machinery. Walking through the offices among typists, prelates, and monsignori, I had a firsthand view of a truly unique bureaucracy. The first section handles all the extraordinary affairs with only twenty-five men. The second handles ordinary affairs with sixty-eight. Including the Chancery of Briefs and the Secretariat of Latin Letters, the count comes to a total of 108 ecclesiastic and

16 lay employees. It is true that the recruiting is still predominantly Italian and it inevitably reflects a certain amount of patronage; every pope and every cardinal introduces his own men. And the Secretariat has broad regional stratifications, each section tending to draw its manpower from Italian provinces still reflecting the territories of the Papal States of another epoch. A sociological examination might indicate a system still tied to the world of the Papal States, but such an indication must not make us overlook the organizational aspects of this phenomenon. Every office chief works best with a staff that he knows well. The directing elements have complete autonomy in their area. The concept of "service" takes care of the rest, coupled with systems perfected by centuries. Today, one can see Chinese and Americans pounding on typewriters there. The transition from the Renaissance to the new world has begun without undermining the efficiency attained in yesterday's world. This bureaucracy, which does not indulge in the rite of the coffee break and which does without the barboys that come and go in comparable Italian offices, is a sort of anomaly in the very heart of Rome. Its "Romanism" is certainly anything but commonplace.

The Secretariat of State, then, is the "political" heart of Roman Catholicism. It is from here that religious policy emerges to become "politics" in the strict sense of the word, since every religious policy conditions or promotes relations between states and the Church. As a bureau, the Secretariat was born in the sixteenth century, as the realm of the "secretarius intimus" and the "cardinal-nephew."[2] It is hence an instrument essentially directed at resolving questions posed by the Renaissance, an instrument at first opposed to the birth of modern states and then enmeshed in the problems of temporal power and its breakdown. As such, it is the Secretariat that has for centuries worked out the political lines of the struggle between the Church and states, and then worked out modern concordat politics in an attempt to end this struggle. But now, with the Secretary of State committed to principles of religious freedom which will necessarily have an impact on the concordats, and with Paul VI speaking for a Church "that asks for nothing more than the liberty to preach the Gospel," there are clear signs that a new vision of policy between Church and states is in the making. Officially, the struggle no longer exists. The concordat form has been divested of certain principles which used to characterize it. Now it remains for the Vatican to work out a new Catholic "political ideology." The problem before us now is to see what indications there are of this new ideology. The indications may be hardly perceptible. But they are there.

CHAPTER VI

The Secretariat of State: The Diplomats

A visit in the Secretariat of State eventually carries one to the sector strictly reserved for foreign policy, which is of course in the renowned "extraordinary affairs" section. Again we are dealing with a branch of the pontifical cabinet, but its structure and lines are unique.[1] In reality, this "section" is a veritable ministry, the ministry of foreign affairs, a ministry only loosely annexed to the Secretariat and operating in direct dependence upon the Secretary of State and the pope. This is understandable, when we consider that the decisions made in this section immediately involve not only diplomatic activities but the general lines of religious policy and the Church's relations with the whole world. The doctrinal positions taken by a pope toward the United Nations, for example, must necessarily be worked out with the help of such a ministry. Catholic "universalism" itself makes of the foreign ministry an organism set off from and overriding the various Curia organisms.

The Section for Extraordinary Affairs has the reputation of being Pacellian. It was ruled until recently by the very Pacellian Cardinal Tardini, and it was then entrusted to men schooled in the Tardinian line. It is consequently often described as the least pliable section, so far as new positions are concerned. This is probably true, at least in part. But it may also be, at least in part, a mere conventional opinion based on the superficial impressions of the uninformed. Entering this section, it is true that you see the signs of the long Pacellian reign: red tapestries impressed with the coat of arms of Pius XII are more numerous here than elsewhere. The atmosphere has a decided stamp of confidentiality and diplomacy. But let us not confuse a diplomatic style, which will not and should not change, with the substance of a policy. After all, it is here that the new diplomatic and international lines behind the positions taken by John XXIII were worked out. In preparing *Mater et Magistra*, mature and deliberate choices had to be made, and they were made in this Pacellian world. Perhaps one day we will come to see the figure of John XXIII less romantically and as that of a pope who was fully aware of what he was doing. When that day comes, we will probably see how certain "overtures," which appeared so isolated, in fact coincided perfectly with the whole posture of Vatican policy. The same men who worked with Tardini in this section went on to develop the Johannine line and are now setting the political policies of Paul VI in motion. Italian observers have speculated heavily in this field and managed to confuse things handsomely. But we need only view it with detachment to make the whole matter clear. In the period of the cold war, Extraordinary Affairs shaped political ideas within the framework of the cold war. In the period following, they worked out new positions. But we shall see this presently, and in context. And this brings us to the men who are the protagonists of this world.

There are two key men in Extraordinary Affairs: Archbishop Antonio Samoré, who is the General Secretary, and Monsignor Agostino Casaroli, who is the Subsecretary.[2] Both are from Emilia in the south Po Valley, and both grew up in the shadow of the Collegio di Piacenza (which is *the* college par excellence for diplomatic clergy, with its roots deep in traditions of seventeenth- and eighteenth-century power and subtlety). These two prelates

symbolize a political action that escapes crude and oversimplify-
ing definitions. Circumspect and Tardinian, Archbishop Samoré
has a vast direct experience with Latin America and eastern
Europe. And it is more than mere chance that his Vice-Secretary
is, on the other hand, a specialist in Far-Eastern questions. Their
close alliance and collaboration with both John XXIII and Paul
VI show clearly how "dialogues" and "closures" are really two
sides of the same coin. This pair of diplomats reflects the major
problems of the Church, which means those of its expansion outside the West as well as those of its relations with Communist
states. They have direct contact with the delicate points of the
present-day world, and hence a new vision of the peace-war
dilemma. To meet them means to dispense with facile schemes
and to embark upon a profoundly different way of reasoning.

Archbishop Samoré received me in a dark drawing room and
then, immediately afterward, I also had a short talk with Monsignor Casaroli in another salon which was decorated, like the
first, with red silk tapestries. I will not dwell too long on the
conversations, which were diplomatic, circumspect, and naturally more revealing in what was not said than in what was said.
Samoré slipped ably back and forth between silence and words.
But he did manage to trace a picture of the principal points of
Vatican foreign policy. "Everything," he said, "turns on three
points. There is that of improving the Church's relations with
the old world. Then we have to develop the new world, like
Latin America, to the maximum, because it has value, because
it is in need, because it will count in the future. And then we
have to work out contacts with the world from which we are still
excluded, in other words with the East and the non-Christian
continents. It's not a matter of accumulating concordats or of expressing a thirst for power, but of pursuing a policy of the Holy
See's universal presence and of having the Church accepted as
a useful adviser among the new states, bringing to them its own
sense of internationalism. Then there are other problems, such
as disarmament. To speak of disarmament doesn't mean anything any more. The new fact in this area is the pope's appeal

made in Bombay which contained the lines for a different view of disarmament, as a complete and international process and as a way of surpassing the logic of the deterrent. . . ." At this point, Samoré cut himself short. He had obviously said too much and so he decided to disappear with a smile.

Immediately thereupon, I found myself face to face with the Subsecretary, Monsignor Agostino Casaroli, the author of the various *modi vivendi* worked out with certain Communist countries. With lively and quick eyes, an open but phlegmatic face, and wearing completely black cassock without any symbol of distinction, Casaroli develops the most advanced line of post-Pacellian foreign policy. "This line has always been confused," he said, "with an ideological truce. I'll give you an example. The USSR has accepted physical coexistence but has refused ideological coexistence. We are working on this terrain because certain international conditions have made it possible to initiate a series of negotiations. From 1940 on, the situation in the East became catastrophic. The papal nunciatures were closed everywhere in the crescendo we are all familiar with, beginning with Estonia and Latvia and ending with the rupture of all relations in Czechoslovakia and Yugoslavia between 1951 and 1952. Then, at the end of the fifties, certain contacts became possible. The first were with the Yugoslavs between 1956 and 1958. Then John XXIII was able to negotiate under different conditions after the posture assumed by Khrushchev in 1961 and on the basis of meetings made possible by the council with bishops from beyond the Iron Curtain. Thus, a policy of rapprochement was delineated between states and not between ideologies, and this policy was continued with my trips to Budapest and Prague in 1963. We try to arrange the naming of bishops, to save what remains of Catholic religious practice, and to obtain provisory *modi vivendi* which permit a minimal presence of the Church in the East."

Monsignor Casaroli stopped. The arrests of priests in Hungary in 1965 give vivid meaning to his words. Against the background of these diplomatic actions, the facts tell us much about the Western-oriented activism of Pius XII and the "new line" of

John XXIII. The last closing of a papal nunciature happened between 1951 and 1953. The beginning of contacts with Yugoslavia took place between 1956 and 1958, even before the Roncalli pontificate. The difficult situation created by the Hungarian revolution interrupted a process which was well under way, in the same way that it interrupted the process of the U.S.A.-USSR thaw. Both processes were resumed afterward. Naturally the personal manner and thrust of John XXIII added the new force of an ecumenical and pastoral view of the Church. But the fact remains that this process of foreign policy was continuous and was, in a sense, prepared in the years of the cold war. While Pius XII refused to receive Cardinal Wyszynski, who had reached a compromise with Poland's Communist premier, Gomulka, he was at the same time laying the foundation for future developments which would bring Wyszynski to Rome. And nothing tells us better than this how risky it is to make distinctions between past and future in this field. Pacellism, Johannism, and Paulism are phases which dovetail into one another; in this light, "overtures" and "closures" are nothing more than facets of politics as "the art of the possible," and we can regard them as different facets of a protracted political action which transcends simple explanations. The present situation is analogous. After the cold war and coexistence, the new phase is unprecedented, more polemical, and focused by Paul VI's famous reference to the "almost impossible dialogue." Nonetheless, Casaroli is a man who works in the realm of the "almost," in whatever margin the historical situation allows.

"It is not the Church," Casaroli said, chuckling, "that determines the phases of history. The Church makes the foreign policy that these phases allow for within the ancient framework of her perfect neutrality." Then he spoke of Hungary, of the difficulties there, of Mindszenty: "this man of granite" who can be "as unyielding as granite." He added precise and sad words on other Hungarian ecclesiastical personalities more friendly toward the regime "who bend like reeds, and are also troublesome—but like reeds in a swamp"; incidental observations, but they are important for understanding a diplomacy which works without ideological truces and requires both flexible resistance and courageous flexibility.

It is anything but easy to draw conclusions from this visit. The few direct but obviously prudent statements which were made hardly permit many safe assertions; but the conversation brings us to a very important and absolutely essential point in our discussion of Vatican diplomatic policy. It is true that new positions, such as that on religious freedom, are finding acceptance in the Secretariat of State. But while this acceptance is taking on concrete form and apparently ringing the death knell of classical concordat politics, it is also true that many old positions are being reconfirmed. The traditional posture of "perfect neutrality" can still be clearly discerned. The techniques of flexibility and adaptation originated by these old positions, and thus tied to the concordat line, are being reinforced. Besides this, one notes a search for new political lines reflected by the words "deterrent," "disarmament," "Eastern relations," etc. And this can only mean a longer delay. We are definitely at the core of Catholic politics, the kernel of the very ideology that lies behind it. We can appreciate here how difficult it is to work out a new and different political ideology even with the declarations of the council, the pope, and the Secretary of State presupposing and apparently even stimulating it.

A visit to the Extraordinary Affairs Section definitely means an examination of relations between state and Church—which in common language means a walk down the blind alley of Church-state relations. Anyone familiar with the problem knows that the origin of all the ideological difficulties of Catholic politics lies in Church-state relations, and that all criticisms of Catholic politics begin at this point. Many observers are surprised that the Church plays the politics of "the vase of clay among the vases of iron"—in other words, of classical concordat politics. They ask themselves why the Vatican has adopted, of all things, a political ideology of flexibility and adaptation in order to realize her political aims. For, like Balzac who dreamed in vain of great affairs, the Church has dreamed of political hegemony for centuries. And instead of realizing her dreams, she has inherited the complications of the present.

It would be pointless to dwell at length on this famous problem.[3] Let it suffice to note that, as an institution, the Church of Rome is the product of a historical choice, the product of that same struggle for survival between state and Church which ended only with the Vatican's loss of temporal power. For centuries before that crisis, the Vatican had opposed the birth of modern, lay, uncommitted, and even Jacobin states; further, she embraced Bossuet's monarchic myth in order to defend the divine conception of authority. Nor indeed could it have been otherwise. For the Church, man is definitely "anterior to the state"; for the Church, the Christian owes a legitimate but limited obedience to the laws of the state. That political posture led the Church to accept "a reactionary fate which republican and democratic Christianity did not have."[4] When the Italian victory over the Papal States in 1870 put an end to the long struggle, the Church had to find other methods of survival. These she found in concordat politics; that is, in replacing her reaction to modern states with a "Catholic diplomacy" based on flexibility and adaptation. This diplomacy functions according to a precise and clear formula. On the one hand it pursues "perfect neutrality" in the interest of concluding concordats, and on the other hand it looks toward using the concordats to contain the power of the states. Even Leo XIII, while first establishing a rationale of neutrality after the debacle of temporal power, made it a point to defend the Catholic thesis of the origins of power against the lay thesis. "The respect due to constituted powers," wrote Leo XIII, "is not to be taken as meaning respect or unlimited obedience to any legislative disposition whatsoever decreed by those powers."

The Church of today, which means the conciliar Church, can therefore be regarded as the product of a second historical choice, and this was concordat politics. Its power is the yield over a long period of "love and hatred" toward the lay states, a period which produced many notorious ambiguities. But these ambiguities are themselves the fruit of an ideology, a precise policy worked out by the Secretariat of State in dealing with the basic problem. In order to survive in the midst of the lay states and to defend Catholicism, the Secretariat of State had anticipated Stalin's question: "How many divisions does the pope have?" Foreseeing the inevitable negative response, the Secretariat worked out the concordat line of diplomacy, traveling the difficult road of an ideology of adaptation. While the Church condemns liberal, Fascistic, and Communistic ideologies, the Secretariat has not hesitated to conclude concordats with states governed by such regimes. Not infrequently, the Secretariat has compromised the line of "perfect neutrality" in order to pursue the purposes of its concordat policy. We need only to think of the papacy of Pius XI when the concordat mania went so far as to "cast on the pope the shadow of an excessive friendship with totalitarian regimes of the right."[5] But all this is very well known, just as it is well known that these concordats proved to be of little avail. For the Church's agreements with Hitler, with Fascist Italy, and her understandings with Argentina, were unable to preclude the anti-Catholicism that was to come in those countries. We record them only to establish that the key to everything lies in the Church-state relations which are determined in this Extraordinary Affairs Section. Concordats were born of the need to survive in the millennial conflict of the Church with the secular world. They are not the fruits of political congeniality or connaturality. They are expressions of a calculation of weakness and an ideology of adaptation. But what other methods are possible? Can a Catholic political ideology exist which is not based on flexibility?

The problem is not "diplomatic" in nature. True, many observers believe that these positions are the fruit of the refusal of the Catholic Church to recognize the decline of its diplomatic power. It is not the Catholic diplomatic body that constitutes the problem. This diplomatic corps enjoys a fame beyond its merits. In a certain sense, its influence is extremely relative. For example, it does not have diplomatic couriers of its own. It employs English, Italian, French, and other couriers, and it is highly probable that many Vatican "secrets" are read before leaving Rome or arriving at their destination. The nunciatures do not have radio stations. And although the Vatican enjoys the reputation of being the "best informed center of the world," we cannot really speak of important diplomatic operations there today. Political cablegrams arrive from missionaries, from papal nuncios, and from envoys. Confidential information may arrive from Catholics all over the world. This intelligence system may facilitate Catholic penetration in the world and the organization of Catholic movements, but it is certainly not a central diplomacy to be feared for its power in contracting agreements. The classical weapons of diplomacy—threats and offers—are definitely not present in Vatican diplomacy. Rome cannot threaten wars or economic embargoes to back up its diplomacy. Excommunication no longer is effective, for reasons obvious to all. Offers of support and alliance, in international agencies for example, are impossible because they conflict with the international interests of the Church herself; thus, supporting a thesis advanced by Paris might evoke negative reactions in Tokyo. For the Vatican, true diplomatic strength can come solely from political and spiritual prestige. And Vatican political prestige is based on four factors. First, all world powers know what the Vatican wants and how far she can go in making concessions. Second, all are familiar with the guarantees of Vatican continuity. Third, all are aware of the Vatican influence on nations of Catholic persuasion (it is a fact that even Sukarno, in the days of his power, habitually stopped in Rome before going to Washington). Finally, the third world, the weak and neutral nations, constitute a new factor today, which for the Vatican acts as political interlocutor when it speaks of peace—in spite of the fact that this interlocutor is variable and apt to disappear tomorrow. Opposed to this prestige, however, there is one last negative factor. The Vatican is an unnatural state, one without borders, without airports, and without real autonomy. As a result, its diplomacy suffers considerably in certain emergencies (as in the years 1940–1945), because it lacks the necessary concrete protections and elementary liberties that independent telephone systems and autonomous air transportation would afford. In view of all this, one can well understand that the ideology of flexibility is, rather than the fruit of astuteness and duplicity, the realistic channeling of a tendency toward compromise and of an irrevocable commitment to ambiguity.

The question arises today as to whether the Vatican can successfully work out another ideology. After the bitter concordat experience with the rightist dictatorships, and after the controversial policies of Pius XII, "perfect neutrality" certainly entered into a new phase with John XXIII, when Vatican universalism took a position clearly transcending all the power blocs. Although this universalism provokes and leaves room for various kinds of diplomatic activities and makes relations with new states possible, it does not change the basic problem. Neither does it change the decision on religious freedom that removes the concordats from the usual angling for privileges. At the end of it all, there is always a question: What political instruments of survival are possible with states if concordats are abandoned? Will future concordats, even if deprived of privilege with respect to religious liberty, be willing to renounce certain claims made against the secular state, such as those made in the field of education? Is a new political ideology possible, one no longer based on Church-state antagonism and the consequent theory of flexibility?

Theologians such as Karl Rahner have already answered this question, saying that the ideology of adaptation must stand, since the Church of Rome regards itself as an "instrument of redemption" and hence as an institution that must spread, survive, and coexist with states in the forms that prove most harmonious with this mission. He says that the only way to avoid adaptations would be to transform Catholicism into a "sect," into a religion without apostolic nuncios, without a diplomatic corps, and without jurisdictional powers. But the separation of Church and state and the reform of the concordat spirit in line with the principles of religious liberty, as they were confirmed by the council, do not necessitate this choice. The failure of the council on the question of "just wars" does not leave much room for departures from the past. But then, a Catholicism that chooses to be a sect is unimaginable, to say the least.

Still, certain attempts are being made to strike out in new directions. John XXIII's declarations to the effect that the Church is above all power struggles constituted the first step in this direction. The hesitation of Benedict XV, and especially of Pius XI, with respect to the League of Nations until yesterday still characterized the Church's posture toward the UN, but was replaced by a completely new attitude with Paul VI's trip to New York. A new reasoning on disarmament which breaks through the logic of the deterrent, an argument for "peace not maintained by fear" means the delineation of a Catholic world policy. Slowly, without proceeding through "overtures" and "ruptures," weaving the universalistic fabric that goes back to Pius X, first through the midst of the rocks of nationalism, then among the "blocs," at times compromising and tormenting itself perhaps, but always taking advantage of the times, the occasions, and the favorable situations, the Church is moving into a supernational political role which will make possible relations with secular states on a new basis. Paul VI's activity for peace during the Vietnam crisis can definitely be considered an act of direct "moral leadership" purged of traditional diplomatic techniques. But the problem now is to know whether such "moral leadership" implies a renunciation of the classical concordat policy which allows for Spanish "adaptations" but which could allow also for adaptations in the East. Then the problem is whether or not this Pauline policy can find men disposed to developing it all the way. The lesson of Pius XII is clear: A pope is not of himself sufficient to assure the Church of a role as a "moral leader"; a methodology and men of conviction who are completely in agreement with the pope are also needed. Moreover, a post-concordatory Catholic political ideology also has to be worked out. The Church of Rome might then—without danger of reducing itself to the status of a sect—entrust its survival to this universalistic leadership. Taking into account the conflict with the civil governments and the concordat policy of appeasement, this seems to be the only new policy possible which would not be based on the principle of flexibility and on the old, and ever contentious, relations between the Church and the states. (At this point, of course, there would arise the problem of so-called Catholic states. The papal Secretariat of State certainly does not share the sentiments of a certain Archbishop of Turin who said, "For heaven's sake, let's forget the whole idea of a Catholic state!"[6])

It is significant to note, in discussing this whole problem, that today we find in the Church a variety of political lines, whereas yesterday there was only uniformity. In those areas where the Church-state conflict has again flared up (as in eastern Europe), the old ideology of adaptation is still followed. But where basic agreement has been reached, the Church is tending toward new positions, such as religious freedom. In the meanwhile, new lines are being developed which point to the consolidation of a direct "moral leadership" for the future.

CHAPTER VII

The Secretariat of State: The Italian Question

We come now to the Ordinary Affairs Section of the Secretariat of State,[1] which brings up the thorny subject of Vatican policy toward Italy. Strictly speaking, this policy ought to be dealt with in the foreign section just described, since Italian relations are a "foreign affair" and since there are sufficient concordatory regulations involved to permit the working out of these relations through regular diplomatic channels. But such is not the case, for history has made of Italy a "special question," and a "special question" comes under Ordinary Affairs. And that is not a play on words; in the Vatican, things very often have the wrong name. Precisely those affairs which are internal and complicated are considered to be "ordinary affairs."

Italy comes under Ordinary Affairs also because these offices are the realm of the Substitute Secretary of State. That is, they are the domain of a key man in the executive branch on whom many responsibilities weigh—indeed on whom "all those duties fall which the pontiff sees fit to entrust to him." The Substitute is one of the pope's cabinet heads and functions directly under the Secretary of State. But his many functions make of him the pontiff's "right arm" for certain problems. The urgent matter, the confidential matter, the official matter—all fall on his shoulders. His task is not the world of protocol, but that of tactical actions, relations that are not formal, or delicate and personal contacts. The Substitute should be thought of as a manager, a personnel chief, an administrator, an organizer. He is also in charge of the archives, takes care of the pope's correspondence, keeps the files between the Secretariat and Catholic Action, between the Secretariat and the Italian Episcopal Conference, and between the pope and the *Osservatore Romano*. In other words, he carries out "any task the pope sees fit to entrust to him." Thus, one can understand how Italian affairs slide out of the Foreign Section to become in practice the Substitute's responsibility.

For the sake of clarity, I will say that my impression of the Substitute's operations confirmed certain theses I had found previously expressed by students of the Church-state question. If what they say is true, if relations with Italy are "anomolous" and "special," it is not because the Holy See pursues the objective of clericalizing the Italian state or because the Holy See seeks to exempt itself from existing legislation so as to bring about a *de facto* confessionalism. On the contrary, these last twenty years of clericalization of Italian life testify to the contrary and show us rather a Holy See, as Jemolo wrote, which acts as a brake on the clericalization and pressure of hierarchy and Catholic politicians "who serve the Church and serve themselves." And so long as state-Church relations are entrusted exclusively to the concordat, clericalization will come and will bring to the Holy See itself all kinds of complications. Such phenomena as the political pressuring of Christian Democrats of the postwar period and the fifties, matched by the well-known interventions of the Pacellian period in the very formation of governments, the behavior of public administrators who have lost sight of the meaning of the state alongside the activism of outside ecclesiastical organs, the collusion between laymen and hierarchy on various juridical or patrimonial capers—all such things have contributed to make the Italian question ever more "special" and "abnormal." I am convinced that the Church and religious organizations have taken up positions abandoned by a society that has forgotten the meaning of the state; but I also had the impression that, in certain circumstances, the Holy See itself today views this clericalization as a burden. Different perspectives and an ever broader internationalism are leading the Holy See today to sever itself from the Italian ties that "Italianize" its policy. I will try to explain what I mean here.

In connection with my talk with Paul VI, I referred to the present pontiff's firm stand against clericalization and in favor of an ever clearer "distinction" between the spheres of influence of the state and the Church. For Paul VI has made certain exemplary statements which indicate his mentality to be less clerical than that of certain lay politicians today. And such statements are not surprising. The recent polemics against Paul VI make us conveniently forget his de Gasperian, anti-Fascist, and liberal-Catholic past, his remoteness from Pacellian positions, his famous discourse on the "Two Romes" in which he invoked, obviously conscious of all the drama it involved, the name of Cavour. But we can well appreciate the suspicions which many observers have of a pope who follows up John XXIII's silence with such unambiguous interventions in Italian affairs as his appeal for order in March, 1966. These observers fear that the Holy See's basic commitment to widening the separation between Church and state in Italy is contradicted by certain facts such as the audience granted to Nicolai Gedda. This is what I had been left with after talking with the men on the Italian side of the Tiber, and those beyond the Tiber who are pursuing policies set by the Secretariat left me with no different impression.

Archbishop Angelo Dell'Acqua, Paul VI's Substitute Secretary of State, received me in his office on the third floor of the Apostolic Palace.[2] The walls of his office are white, without tapestries, and the office is full of telephones. Dell'Acqua dominates the scene with his gigantic clear-eyed personality and his abrupt but honest and direct manner. I know it is inexact to put it this way, but my impression of Dell'Acqua was of an open and decisive northern Italian executive. His activistic figure certainly evidenced none of the ambiguities of traditional diplomatic circumlocution and prudence. He is often spoken of as a socialistically-inclined bishop who set the center-left movement in operation. But we must not forget that Dell'Acqua was Substitute under two other popes before Paul VI. "They think of my social background," he said, "then they identify me with the left." Discussing Paul VI's "interventions" and John XXIII's "disengagement," Dell'Acqua said, "I think there is too much talk, and too little real knowledge of how things really stand. There are disengagements which really amount to interventions that no one ever knows about. And there are interventions that turn out to be *de facto* disengagements. If they would only wait a while before judging us! Certainly there was a Johannine line of nonintervention so far as men and activity are concerned, and that line did aim at limiting our interest in public morality, education, and youth. And I think that line is still in effect. Certain recent interventions were occasioned by emergency situations caused by others, not by us. I am referring to *The Deputy* and all the rest. We simply try to counter emergency situations with our own emergency until new possibilities open up." The conversation then turned to organizational matters, the eighty thousand telegrams the Secretariat receives every year, the 380,000 transactions handled every year, etc. When we got back to the main issue, the Substitute looked me straight in the eye and said, "Look, the line you call 'Johannine' is still in full effect. That's the absolute truth."

Summarizing such a rapid and "coded" conversation, I would say that there are two important facts behind Paul VI's "interventions," and they are the massive offensive of *The Deputy* and the crisis in the Christian Democratic left. The Church had not been subjected to such violent attack in many years, and having been attacked while the Catholic left was in a state of crisis created a state of emergency. Nevertheless, there has been a continuous development of the Johannine policy of disengagement, as is borne out by the way Paul VI interprets the concordat, for example. I believe that Paul VI's position on the concordat is indisputably much more advanced than those of the popes that preceded him. Paul regards it as dangerous to upset the delicate and precious equilibrium of the present concordat; however, he does not exclude the possible usefulness of reviewing the whole arrangement. The fact is, certain revisions will never be obtained by exposing this equilibrium to political and subversive attack, and it is increasingly clear that the Socialist and other positions which attack the concordat problem with such weapons as *The Deputy* are not being effective in obtaining a disengaged Vatican and in getting Italy out of the "special affairs" area.

This brings us to the men responsible for expressing the orientations of the Vatican Secretariat of State. The key instrument of these orientations is Catholic Action; and the new General Assistant for Catholic Action, Bishop Franco Costa, who is the link between the Holy See and this important lay organization, confirmed the impressions I have already described. Chosen by Paul VI, Bishop Costa is a Genoese whose position definitely differs from that of his compatriot, Cardinal Siri. He told me: "There are new lines today which receive their inspiration and drive from the council, and we are following them. These lines call for a transition from a position of polemicism to one of presence—fewer accusations, and more presence in the political area. How is this presence in politics expressed? We say it is in the formula "respect and autonomy" toward the Holy See. Respect, because we ask of Catholics engaged in politics an unambiguous conformity with Catholic principles; autonomy, because autonomy means two things. On the one hand, it means to serve the Church without serving oneself in doing so; thus we would put a stop to the clericalization of Italian life. On the other hand, autonomy means acting in harmony with principles without the obligation of making choices determined by vested interests. Naturally the Vatican has to promote the line of Catholic unity. But this unity has to be expressed differently and must not violate autonomy. The recent case of the election of Giuseppe Saragat, a Socialist, as President of Italy, is a concrete example of a call to unity with full respect for autonomy. The Vatican politically was uncommitted to the choice of a non-Catholic or a Catholic; it asked only for unity in the decision. This is how I would define the concept of disengagement. It is not indifference. It is respect for political autonomy."

Bishop Costa then clarified the position of the Secretariat on the dialogue with Italian Communism. "The polemic presents this problem in a false light. It is said that, before Paul VI, Catholics had an autonomy which his interference with the dialogue has now limited. The truth is, he did not repress this autonomy, but gave it the definition it needed. Paul VI is in favor of religious discussion with all in the spirit of John XXIII, and he has affirmed the Johannine principle that there are seeds of truth and good everywhere. But when this religious discussion becomes a monopoly of Communists and is clearly motivated by political interests, thus limiting the dialogue to the choice of only one interlocutor, and when that interlocutor is represented exclusively by a party about which the Church has its deep and understandable apprehensions, then it simply has to be made clear that this was not the dialogue desired and welcomed by all."

After Bishop Costa, I had another meeting with the Cardinal of Milan, Giovanni Colombo, who, together with two other cardinals, presides over the Italian Episcopal Conference, which was until recently directed by Cardinal Siri. The Conference of Bishops is an essential instrument tied to the Secretariat of State, and it is apt to produce many new positions even in the political area. "What we have to face," the cardinal told me, "is an organizational problem. In Italy, the Episcopal Conference is still a muzzled organism. We have to increase its representative capacity and give it the same responsibilities that these conferences have in other countries. The time has surely come for the Italian bishops to deal with the Italian questions and leave the Holy See free to cope with its universal responsibilities."

On the basis of these talks I think we can deduce certain things. The Holy See is presently pursuing a policy of "disengagement" as far as Italy is concerned, and if I call it a controlled policy I think it will be evident and understandable to all. It hinges on the clear position of Paul VI who, as no pope before him, is conscious of the concept of the distinction of powers. This disengagement is being defined now in terms of the autonomy of Catholics and not of a renunciation of the right to speak on questions of principle. However, instruments such as the Episcopal Conference are being prepared which will certainly normalize the situation by shifting the weight of the interventions from the pope to the Italian bishops—as it is in France or Belgium. Whether it is a question of political expediency or of matters of principle, the trend is toward improvement and toward regression. Obviously, predictions are impossible in this area. The question now is how to interpret certain acts of Paul VI, such as the audience granted to the civic committees. Whenever I asked about these things, I was assured that these acts do not represent the contradiction of a political line. Paul VI did not perform them as "relaunchings," but only as a "recuperation" of men and forces disoriented by the recent transition from the active engagement of yesterday to the controlled disengagement of today. Here, too, the Vatican is changing. There are winners and there are losers in today's Catholicism. This pope has inherited a Catholic people that recent history has divided into winners and losers. And it seems to be his desire to reunite them and to transform them into Catholics without animosity and bitterness on either side.

CHAPTER VIII

The Secretariat of State: Finances

Finding oneself in the Secretariat of State, it becomes natural to wish to acquire some explanation of Vatican finances. Admittedly, it is not a question related to the council or the new lines of the Church. But the subject is extremely controversial and no serious discussion of the changing Vatican can possibly overlook it. The finance problem is tied to the methods used in running a government. It is an expression not of political but economic "temporal" power. To take the confusion and mystery out of it seems to be an urgent obligation of the central power of the Church. The opening up of dialogues, the fundamental transition from a Church which distrusts today's values to a "welcoming" Church, and certain shifts in religious policy inevitably imply a revision of the Church's stand regarding money—or, better still, a revision of the idea public opinion has of the Church's financial affairs. The Vatican's idea of money may very well be basically charitable or purely instrumental for religious purposes, but the Vatican does little to convince public opinion of this fact. With the world news media from *Time* to the *Economist* speaking of the financial mystery of the Holy See, numerous Catholics feel the need of a change in this sector. At a certain point, one's "philosophy of money" enters even into doctrinal reasoning.

Let me admit from the start that I am not qualified to deal with this problematic area as a specialist or authority. The truth is that this was the real "dark zone" of my trip to the Vatican, although I hold that to be more the effect of confusion than of bad will, more the result of indecision than of malice. Personally, I am convinced that the Vatican economic mechanism is wrapped up in what economists call "plutocratic incapacity"—a psychological phenomenon similar to that of the priest who runs away from life but who is at the same time intent on changing it. I think the Vatican machine follows a devil-money dialectic which incites to excess and to deficiency, which turns a scorn for money into a cult of money, which nourishes sagacity in naïveté, and which creates simple techniques that become able techniques and creates adroitness that leads only to complications. But my personal opinions do not count any more than the opinions of those who say the Vatican is a victim of the "profit cult." We are all free to consider frustrations as cults, or vice versa, just as we are free to regard economic activity in a Church as positive or negative. But this does not concern us here, whereas what I am going to examine concerns all of us. I know very little. What little I know cannot be proved. I have seen little, I understood even less, and I do not want to use secondhand information or repeat things that are common knowledge.[1] In other words, I represent the public-opinion problem that the Vatican is going to have to face.

At the bottom of the problem of Vatican finances there is definitely a problem of public opinion. Aside from clerical and anticlerical opinions and moral conflicts concerning wealth, there still remains a question of clarity, even when we grant that financial affairs and operations inevitably require a certain amount of secrecy. Naturally, the Vatican adjusted itself in the past to various historical conditions and operated with the methods it then deemed best. But why should it now refuse to operate accordingly in an era which calls for other methods? No one disputes the fact that, from the economic point of view, the Church is to be regarded as a "moral foundation." And it is certainly legitimate for the Church to maintain this moral foundation with securities investments, financial maneuvers, and other normal techniques used to keep all foundations financially active and growing. Further, it is only just that, as a moral foundation, the Church seek to obtain such fiscal exonerations, facilitations, and protections as are conceded to all foundations. But this can be justified only on the grounds of an open organization and the administrative techniques that this implies: the availability of the balance sheets, the declaration of capital invested, and the financial statement. Then there is the ethical problem of keeping false or correct balance sheets. But it is easy to imagine that this problem does not arise for "moral" institutions—at least in those countries whose tax policy favors foundations.

The Vatican obviously finds it hard to present itself to public opinion in the garb of a moral foundation. And this makes it impossible for the Vatican to establish a legitimate economic policy toward states. It is true that many Italian political parties assume a position of opposition to the Vatican and that this opposition seriously conditions the Church's posture in this area. But it is conceivable that such opposition would diminish under the pressure of an informed and convinced public opinion if the Vatican were to abandon certain of its methods. Today the Vatican has only the disadvantages of the financial "mystery" and of its confused policy. Figures quoted only evoke images of avarice and the "gold cult" precisely because they are not framed as terms of the balance sheet. The Vatican often drags along in a sort of informational narcosis, spreading the idea that her figures are not accurate. But since the true figures are unknown, the so-called "false figures" remain the only frame of reference public opinion has. It would be different if, alongside certain real estate holdings, notice were given of the Vatican expenses for churches, leper colonies, seminaries, schools, charities, benefits, etc. It is all very well that the Vatican is above suspicion and that its "sacredness" is too exalted to be subjected to the obligation of denying accusations levied against it. This is not the issue. The issue is that of a dangerous logic. The figures are circulating, and that "sacredness" is not being defended.

Time magazine has written that Vatican holdings amount to some ten or fifteen billion dollars. In 1952, an Italian weekly said that the Vatican treasury is the second in the world, having a gold reserve of seven trillion lire (eleven billion dollars), which would make it three times that of England. *Time* has always maintained that the Vatican holds stocks in Italian corporations to the tune of a trillion lire ($1.6 billion) or 15 per cent of the shares quoted in Italian stock exchanges. While these figures flutter about the cupola of St. Peter's, the Catholic is given no creditable information or any official report on the reason for such large holdings. It can be admitted that preaching the word of Christ incurs an expense and that this expense cannot be exposed to the ups and downs of material charity but has to be stabilized by the active column of a fixed property income. It can also be accepted that the dimensions of a universal Church require a reserve three times that of England. We can recognize as legitimate an "accumulation of capital" in institutions serving religious ends. But the Vatican says nothing of the "liabilities" column to contradict what its enemies say about the "assets" column. Neither can we accept as adequate the propaganda published in the communiqués sent out to the missions about the works of charity, new churches, etc.

The dispute about Italian dividend declarations and "Vatican tax fraud" comes down to nothing more than a failure to keep public opinion informed. The arguments are well known, so I won't dwell on them. Italy issued a law on dividend declarations in December, 1962. Through diplomatic channels, the Italian Embassy was informed that the Holy See considers it "advisable" not to apply the law to dividends paid to Vatican organisms. In an exchange of notes, the Holy See was informed that the Italian government was in agreement. But later this "tax privilege" met with resistance by the Socialists in the government. The easy yielding of the Christian Democrats who agreed to the facilitation without even asking the Vatican to publish a clear explanation was matched by the duplicity of the Socialists who opposed what was done but avoided a clash in order to save the center-left. And so, a serious and basic question was left unresolved, providing only the anticlerical press with the advantage of uncovering it and talking of "tax frauds." The Vatican invoked legislative precedents and the exemptions obtained in 1942 within the framework of concordat agreements. The adversaries replied that such exemptions were the questionable fruits of Fascist favoritism. It is obvious that everyone stands to gain by a clear solution. The Vatican would gain in asking the state to recognize its status as a "moral foundation." The Christian Democrats would gain in not having to deal under the table and not involving the Church in behind-the-scenes politics. And the opponents would gain in not covering over with one hand what they disapprove with the other.

It is surely not easy for the Vatican to present itself in a new way to public opinion. Vatican financial policy is tied to the traditional political ideology and to the Secretariat of State's favorite formula whereby the Church should not make compromises but adapt itself to reality. The necessity of saving the "institution," even with secret reservations, prevails over the necessity of finding new methods. At the base of all the methods are the Secretariat's conceptions of policy which go back to Leo XIII. But we have already mentioned this and we will speak of it again very shortly, by way of conclusion. In any case, the problem of money is not merely a subject for anticlerical satire, but a serious matter which touches on general policy. This problem can be understood in terms of what Hans Küng referred to as the Vatican's "double commitment." Money is only another aspect of the dilemma between "message" and "institution" which is so hard to resolve, but which can be resolved here also, as Karl Rahner says, if Catholic Christianity became a "church of active members" and hence, in substance, "a sect." However, though we do not object to slow developments in some areas, the postponement of a reform in this sector is hard to justify. It

is not a question of "pauperizing" the Church, but of legitimitiz-
ing its wealth like that of any moral foundation. Certain elements
in the Secretariat are aware of this exigency. But men and structures complicate the attempt to make decisions about it.

My limited experience does not permit me to judge the organisms, the persons involved, or the centers of power capable
of changing or not changing the situation. Taking up this problem, however, I found that the men in charge of money in the
Vatican are inevitably the most unshakable advocates of the old
Leonine concepts in the Secretariat. They are often considered
to be qualified precisely because they possess an "administrative" understanding of religion, while objectively their qualifica-
tion is really only relative—which means good when compared
with that of other priests, but inferior when compared with that
of lay financial experts. It would be dishonest to deny having
interviewed what I had to regard as storybook characters in the
economic offices, priests who (like their anticlerical critics) turn
finance into an affair of romance and mystery, priests who think
of themselves as magicians. For these priests, such words as interest, investment, profit, etc., take on an Aesopian meaning, and
the money-devil dialectic turns into fairy tales for children. But
these are borderline cases, characters of administrative folklore.
The general line is less astute and at the same time less naïve,
less innocent, less country-style. Vatican finances are really handled elsewhere: somewhere outside, or in a place inaccessible
from the inside.

Many prelates in the Curia are aware that the economic problem is tied to public opinion, but they believe in the old recipe
that "it is best that people think the Vatican is not too rich and
not too poor. If they think it is too rich, they lose their faith in
it. If they think it is too poor, they lose their respect for it." And
so they think the question of public opinion is best solved by
absolute secrecy, or the reverse of the policy of German and
other Catholics who publish the diocesan financial statements
for whoever is interested. But beyond this there is a more important problem of "structures." The economy of the Holy See is

still the labyrinth it always was and in which even the pope gets lost. There are double and triple administrations like that of the Secretariat of State, that of the Possessions of the Holy See, the Special Administration, etc. Commissions of cardinals, "fiduciaries," laymen, various counselors, etc., conduct different policies which cross over one another and which mix good administrations with bad, and wise disinterested advice with wild speculation. The Vatican is thus the beneficiary and the victim of an old structure that has the advantages of secrecy but the disadvantages of depending on distorted information. I will not say how this world works because I do not know myself. But the fact remains that the pontificate of Paul VI is at least inclined to a renovation of the "system." In order to present itself to the world as a foundation, the Vatican must first study and resolve the confusion in its financial affairs, and then formulate a policy. In this connection, there was talk in 1965 of an "economic prefecture" or a sort of ministry of finance which would be capable of keeping books and using new methods. And I believe that if this becomes a reality, it would free Catholics of all their complexes on the question. A "transparent Vatican" is one of the innovations that are coming out of these years of transition. Needless to say, it would turn even more swords into plowshares.

CHAPTER IX

The Secretariat of State: The Real Deputy

The famous and inaccessible Vatican Archives was the final object of my visit to the Secretariat of State. I was accompanied
there by the Substitute. We reached a sunlit room high above the
roof of the Apostolic Palace where Chinese, German, Italian, and
other priests were at work in the midst of piles of fascicles and
documents. This was the antechamber of the archives proper.
Then, a huge vertical well with balconies, little stairways, and
metal grilles opened up and gave me the impression of being in
the hull of a ship, full of automatic gratings and armored stacks.
Everything is ordered and protected in the stacks, with completely isolated sections where the second door won't open until
the first is closed. Descending to the different levels of the well,
one sees lined up the secret documents of the various papacies.
"Here are the most important documents of Pius XII," said the
Substitute, pointing to some white binders with backs stamped
in gold. "Some are of extreme importance in connection with
Nazism and the Jews. We'll never make them public under the
pressure of certain ignoble attacks, but we are preparing a series
of publications to be printed when the opportune moment comes
for the Church."

The first series of these documents has been published since my visit.[1] It appeared in the very year (1965) of those "ignoble attacks" and the date selected for publication coincided with the closing of the council. There is no doubt that considering such a date as opportune is particularly significant. It is not Vatican tradition to publish secret papal papers. The archives have been officially closed since 1846 except for very limited permissions. Therefore to publish "everything" connected with Pius XII is an act which goes "against the system" and can only be understood as a council gesture. As a matter of fact, these documents reveal more than specific actions and postures of Pius XII. They exemplify techniques of government, they underline certain lines of Catholic policy, and they reach into the very foundations of the ideology on which that policy was constructed. To draw up and publish a balance sheet which is certainly not fully positive and which poses certain problems for the future may very well mean a rethinking of the policy of the Secretariat of State, or a decision of the Secretariat to reflect on itself. To say that the collection is an answer to the play *The Deputy* is too simple. It is definitely much more, but it is "also" an answer to *The Deputy* in the measure with which it offers to the Catholic hierarchy itself a critical analysis of the policy of the Secretariat, matching libel with history, the mutilated and slandering assertion with the complete documentation, the political attack with the scientific study. The thesis proposed by the adversaries (Pius XII's culpable silence before the Nazi persecutions) is shaken by the public consultation of all the diplomatic documents, thus initiating more a critical process than a self-defense. As a matter of fact, a self-criticism of the Vatican apparatus itself can be detected in this gesture. But we will come to this in another connection. Let us first of all see how the true deputy emerges from the Vatican Archives.

The documentation begins with March 3, 1939, which is the day after the election of Pius XII to the papacy. The relations between the Church and Nazism is touched on, a question to which serious historical studies have been dedicated, such as those of Ritter and Lewy.[2] Then follows the day-by-day posture of Pius XII toward the war, toward German aggression in Poland, toward Italian neutrality, and toward the Nazi violence in Belgium and Holland. On the whole, Pius XII appears as a pope "conditioned" by either state-Church relations or the governing techniques of the Secretariat. The situation was already difficult when he came to the throne. But, as is clear also from the memoirs of Count Dalla Torre, Pius XII was animated by a desire to repair the rift between Pius XI and Fascism.[3] His posture toward Germany therefore quickly jelled in certain policies. In Germany (as Lewy has documented) the German bishops declared again after 1933 the incompatibility of Catholicism and Nazism. At the same time, after Pius XI's famous encyclical (*Mit brennender Sorge*) condemning National Socialism, anti-Catholic persecution became acute. The episcopate found it necessary to make many concessions. The clergy opposing the Nazi neopaganism and the sterilization and euthanasia campaigns suffered painfully, as both Lewy and Ritter point out and document. But, in the face of such a situation, which was a prelude to the horrors of the war of ideologies, Pius XII formulated certain classical diplomatic policies in the tradition of Leo XIII. Toward the war he chose the policy of perfect neutrality which had been worked out for national wars. Toward the Nazi ideology, he continued the doctrinal opposition of Pius XI. Toward the German military activities he chose a policy of equally classical and traditional protests against violations of natural and international law, without disturbing the Church's position of perfect neutrality. And toward the German episcopate Pius XII assumed an equally classical posture based on the formula of the just war versus the unjust war. This doctrine is of course well known as the sore point of Catholic policy. In spite of the fact that all theologians agree that no war can be just for both sides, the doctrine continues to stand, producing in every conflict the double track of Roman ambiguity. The Vatican upper levels declare themselves neutral and hence abstain from judgments regarding justice or injustice. But in reality it leaves the national episcopates on their own to decide concerning the "justice" of the war being waged by their particular country, and the episcopates generally act according to the Catholic doctrine of preaching faithfulness to legitimate power. The result was that each episcopate supported its own country's war, with the French bishops supporting France's war, the German bishops supporting the German war, etc.; and alongside of the Vatican neutrality there emerged the biased commitment of many bishops. Hence, everywhere there was the ambiguity of a double position, with the ancient drama of the pope being divided between two policies and accused of duplicity. And we find the same policy, the same drama, accepted by Pius XII and leaving the German episcopate the liberty of supporting or opposing the "just" Nazi war and reserving "neutrality" and the defense of the "violated" to the Holy See. This is another typical Vatican posture worked out in the days of national wars, before this age of ideological wars.

The documents delineate exactly the month-by-month development of these political lines. They give the lie to the slanderous thesis against Pius XII (that he was pro-Nazi and blameworthy). But in no way do they develop the image of a pope in the position of an unconstrained "moral leader" capable of transcending the methods of the Secretariat of State, as did Benedict XV during World War I in pronouncing his unmitigated condemnation of "the needless bloodbath."[4] Pius XII worked with the subtle technique of negotiation, "omissions," "prudence," etc. He upheld his own right to speak and was not "silent," as the discreditation would have it. But it is the "classical" or "Leonine" right to speak. As even the sharply critical Lewy admits, the figure of Pius XII imposes itself as that of a pope who would not keep silent, although his word was conditioned by Catholic political ideology, by the policy of the Church following its usual flexible course and adapting itself to the course of events and preaching the ancient principles of obedience to authority. The result is that his word appears out of place in a struggle where authority realizes such extremes as Nazi ideology, gas chambers, and deportation on a vast scale. Even when he shows courage in deploring the violence perpetrated against neutrals, it sounds unnatural and ill-timed in the face of the tragic destiny of man who discovers that, as a result of the ideological wars, the dilemma of his obedience to authority makes him responsible not merely for national wars but even for criminal catastrophes and mass offenses. My impression is that Pius XII was more irrelevant than silent.

But let us take a look at history as it really was. There are moments when we will find that not infrequently the minutest detail, when magnified under the microscope, reveals the true drama of the deputy.

In the first phase (autumn, 1939) Pius XII encounters the problem of "silence" about the German aggression on Poland. And for many reasons, he resolves it with extreme caution. In the first place Pius XII does not agree with Pius XI[5] and considers himself a "diplomatic" instrument in reserve for limiting the war and bringing about an armistice. Secondly, he is thinking of Italian neutrality and does not wish to eliminate so valuable an interlocutor as Mussolini. Thirdly, he does not want to make the situation of German Catholics more difficult. For these reasons, he refuses to intervene too early in accord with English and French requests. At the same time, he clearly does not want to accept Mussolini's request to appeal to the Poles to induce them to concessions toward the Germans. Pius XII does not want to encourage the Nazis with another Munich. He lets the nuncio in Warsaw attempt a last mediation. Ultimately, he stands before the conflict, in a sense "silent" and in another sense "outspoken." But the nature of this silence and of this outspokenness becomes evident to all by August, 1939. As a matter of fact, when an appeal is requested from the pope to incite the Poles to concessions toward the Germans, a note comes from Tardini to Maglione on August 30 which says: "The initiative toward Poland is not without danger. Munich consists in precisely this. Hitler shouted, threatened, and obtained what he wanted. So also for Danzig. Hitler's shouts and threats would obtain, with the help of the

Holy See, the return of Danzig to the Reich." The Vatican objectives are hence the "preservation of peace and the saving of Poland." At the same time, a condemnation of Nazism is excluded in order to protect Poland, as is demonstrated by two notes dated August 28 and 30 signed by Monsignori Montini and Tardini. Montini writes: "The French ambassador sends this article. In a conversation this morning he added that it would be very opportune to have a word or a public gesture from the Holy See in direct support of Poland even before it enters into the great trial that is impending." Tardini adds: "His Holiness says that this would be too much. We cannot forget that there are forty million Catholics in the Reich. What would they be exposed to after such an act by the Holy See? The pope has already spoken to Osborne, and has made this perfectly clear." The conclusion was that Poland was invaded without a complaint from the pope, not even a complaint against the "needless bloodbath." Only in a cautious encyclical on October 20, 1939, does Pius XII take a position, pronouncing these words: "The blood of countless human beings, even noncombatants, lifts up a heart-rending cry of mourning over a nation so beloved as is Poland." But he will never attach to the expression "heart-rending cry" the force of a condemnation. The documents show that in his talk with Ribbentrop in 1940 he made it clear that his words of compassion ("the small invaded nation") at Christmas, 1939, referred to Finland, not Poland. The cautious objective of Pius XII as the conflict opened up was more that of sympathizing in the Polish suffering than of denouncing Nazi violence.

In the second phase (winter, 1939, to spring, 1940), Pius XII conditioned his silence and words regarding the problem of Italian neutrality and Fascist blackmail. The *Osservatore Romano* took an openly pacifist stand which testified to the pope's position as a "moral leader." At the same time, Pius avoided a rupture with Mussolini who, it was hoped, was still not completely lost. In general the documents do not indicate any endorsement of the Nazi-Fascist war. Relations between Italy and the Holy See were good. In the wake of the concordat, Ciano, the Italian

foreign minister, and Father Tacchi Venturi, the Jesuit who maintained the official relations between Mussolini and the Secretariat
of State, continually repeated that Mussolini would remain neutral. In his hope for a diplomatic solution, Pius XII rejected other
requests for an anti-German intervention and even rejected Latvia's proposal that the Holy See organize the unification of the
neutral nations into a bloc ("because it is not clear," writes
Maglione, "how such an initiative would be received among the
other nations concerned"). When it became clear that attempts
at mediation had failed, Pius XII wrote a personal letter to Mussolini on April 24 and stated frankly that his diplomatic measures
had been useless. The letter was full of flattering expressions and
praise for the neutral line maintained up to then. Pius XII uses
the familiar form of address (the *tu*), blesses and flatters, but
opposes the decision that has already been made. "We know
your noble efforts, efforts with which you wished first of all to
avoid and then to localize the war," writes the pope, "and never
doubting your persevering efforts to realize the policy to which
you have committed yourself, we beg the Lord to assist you in
such a grave and serious hour . . . and we express the ardent
desire that Europe be saved from even worse destruction through
your initiative, your firmness, and your true Italian spirit. And in
particular that our and your beloved country be protected from a
grave disaster." But Mussolini's response on April 30 was cold
and businesslike. For all the admiring phrases of the pope, he
wasted no expression of respect for the pope's action, and in substance he suggested that the Holy See refrain from mixing in
strictly Italian affairs. He expressed his gratitude with formality
("kindly receive, most blessed Father, my deep gratitude for the
expressions in my behalf which were contained in the letter you
[the formal expression *voi*] deigned to address to my person")
and then turns the pontiff's praises into a sort of approval of his
actions: "Your acknowledgement of my efforts gives me much
satisfaction." But then he informed the pope that French and
English indiscretion started the war and that peace was impossible. "I understand," said Mussolini, "your desire that it be given to

Italy to avoid war. This has been possible until the present date, but I can in no way guarantee that it will continue so to the end." Then Mussolini gives the pope a lesson in history. "The history of the Church, and it is you who have taught me this, has never accepted the doctrine of peace for peace's sake, peace at all costs, peace without justice." And the letter closed with "the expression of my devoted respects" in a manner suggesting the end of the dialogue. Thus, Pius was worse off than before. The pope had unmistakably issued Mussolini a license of pacifist legitimacy, and in exchange ended up without the interlocutor in whom he had placed so much trust.

Pius' reaction was to become more prudent in the future. Being requested from all sides to intervene with condemnations and excommunications against Hitler and Mussolini and with anticipatory denunciations of the invasion of Belgium and other neutral countries, Pius XII preferred to wait. As Cardinal Maglione explained to the nuncio in Paris: "The Holy Father has done whatever he could, even addressing a letter to the head of the Italian government. Unfortunately, he does not see what else is possible beyond constant opposition, and diffusion of the *Osservatore Romano*. Countless troublesome incidents in regard to the *Osservatore Romano* continue." A note of Monsignor Montini, dated May 19, finally described the real situation, after the visit of Italy's Ambassador Attolico to the Vatican. In response to the Vatican's protests against recent confiscations of the *Osservatore Romano*, the ambassador "definitely admits that the distribution of the newspaper in Italy is practically forbidden," and he confirms "how the Italian government, having decided to enter into the war, cannot allow to exist any voice not in conformity with the rest of the Italian press."

Pius XII's prudence becomes even more visible in certain corrections made in his Christmas Message of 1939. In the first draft he had written: *"The living space of one nation must never mean the death sentence of another."* But then he crossed out *"living space"* and wrote *"the will to live."* These are the ideological precautions of a man whose peace-serving judgment also contains the anti-Communist ideal ("the war will exhaust the nations and increase the force and techniques of disorder which are only biding their time to deal the telling blow to Christian Europe"). But it is also the prudence of a man who wants to avoid reprisals. Italian neutrality was becoming less and less certain, and Fascist attacks against the *Osservatore Romano* were under way. In April, 1939, Bottai summoned the nuncio, Borgognini Duca, and reiterated Italian protests against the *Osservatore* for "casting in a rosy light whatever touches on France and England." Bottai informed him that, in the last sitting of the Chamber of Fasces, one of the members had spoken of the Vatican as "a chronic appendix of Italy." As it comes out in the documents published by the archives, Borgognini replied that "the *Osservatore* cannot support Italian policy and that the Holy See cannot be Fascist." Nevertheless, in view of the incidents of 1939 (confiscated papers, *Osservatore* delivery trucks blocked), the situation seems to have become even more delicate. Lord Perth, the English ambassador to Italy, and Lord Halifax, the English foreign minister, expressed their admiration for the *Osservatore* and asked the pope "to do everything possible to maintain Italian neutrality," assuring him that England did not desire the downfall of Mussolini." Pius XII now moved very cautiously, for two reasons: first, to stave off reprisals already under way; and secondly, to keep Mussolini "on the hook" up to the end in order to win him over to neutrality. He was to pay dearly for this diplomatic illusion. Still, these things do not add up to total silence. For instance, When the Low Countries were invaded, Pius XII did speak out—and it is interesting to observe how he did speak, in what terms, and with what methods.

The third phase (spring and summer of 1940) explains how Vatican political ideology prevailed over the sentiments of "protest" expressed by the pope and even by Tardini. The documents focus directly on the theme of Hochhuth's *The Deputy,* and we should peruse them very carefully because they reveal how Pius XII and his collaborators, twenty-five years ago, clearly viewed the problem of "silence" which is at the base of anti-

Pacellian accusations. These documents contain a sort of bitter prophecy of future defamations and insulting recriminations. There is the consciousness of living a drama (the "Christian drama") of which history would one day demand an explanation.

In the summer of 1940, the most dramatic months of the conflict, Italy decided on war while Nazi aggression was involving thitherto neutral countries in the fray. With all hope lost and all diplomatic possibilities exhausted, the world again turned to the pope in the desperate illusion that his word could stop Hitler's tanks. Thus, on the morning of May 10, as a telegram from Nuncio Micara in Brussels informed the Vatican of the beginning of the tragedy ("about four o'clock this morning German army invaded Belgium without declaration of war and without any diplomatic procedure whatever"), Pius XII found himself with the problem of having to make a statement. Charles Roux, the ambassador of France to the Holy See, requested an audience for that same morning to repeat his bid for an intervention by the pope. Myron Taylor, Roosevelt's representative, the Belgian ambassador, and the foreign minister of England added themselves to the list. The telegram of the French government made an explicit request for "a pontifical protest denouncing this abominable violation of law and morality." And in commenting on these facts Cardinal Maglione observed: "This French communiqué was immediately sent by me to the Holy Father. His Holiness telephoned to tell me that he would receive the ambassador and would suspend the other audiences. On that very afternoon His Holiness personally prepared three telegrams"—typing them himself. "With those telegrams His Holiness thought to forestall the other diplomats by presenting them with a *fait accompli.*"

It is useful to analyze this protest against the invasion because it throws light on the different positions of the protagonists in the Secretariat of State with respect to the French request and the subsequent English request for a "public and formal condemnation of the Nazi aggression on the part of the Holy See." That day of May 10, 1940, epitomizes the drama of *The Deputy* down to the smallest details. In the face of the French request, Pius XII decided to take the initiative. As Vatican documents bring out, he immediately communicated to the Substitute Secretary of State, Montini, the idea of having the Secretariat prepare a letter from the pope to the Secretary of State, with the objective of condemning the Nazi aggression. Thus "at about 1:15 P.M. Montini communicated this wish to Maglione and Tardini." But the proposal gave rise to two reactions. Maglione was in favor of a communiqué to be published in the *Osservatore Romano,* whereas Tardini, the assistant secretary, simply prepared the draft of the letter desired by Pius XII. And it is not difficult to divine from the documents how the Maglione line differed from that of Tardini. The cardinal wrote in his rough draft: "In expressing our deep sympathy with the suffering nations, we cannot refrain from deploring the violations of international and natural law which fill every noble heart with unspeakable pain." Tardini, however, wrote in his draft of the pope's letter: "With great sorrow we have witnessed the suffering and anguish of small nations which, after having made every attempt to preserve peace, were overrun one after the other against their will by the all-devouring avalanche, guilty only of being weak and of exposing their neutral territory to the possibility of offense and defense by the strongest belligerent nations. And today, when we see three industrious, tranquil and peace-loving nations struck down without provocation, attacked without just cause, we cannot refrain from lifting up our voice to deplore once again the iniquity and injustice of this act." Thus, Tardini's letter was a total and courageous condemnation of the entire Nazi war and a solemn defense of the neutrals, whereas Maglione's draft contained only an attenuated deploration of violations. We can see clearly the alternatives before Pius XII.

In the afternoon of that same day, the pope made his choice. He made it in line with the traditional technique of power which requires a pope to remain the mediator between extremes, between opposed points of view. It is also an expression of his temperament as the ruler of a Church who wished only executors, not collaborators. Pius XII rejected both Tardini's letter and Maglione's note. He sat down himself at the typewriter to write to Leopold of Belgium, Wilhelmina of Holland, and Charlotte of Luxembourg, telegrams which constituted a courageous censure of Hitler but which at the same time avoided the formula of a solemn and "formal" condemnation. In his message to Leopold of Belgium, Pius XII said: "In this hour when, for the second time, against its will and rights, the Belgian people sees its territory exposed to the cruelty of war, we send assurance of our paternal affection. We pray God that this trial may conclude with the return of full liberty and independence in Belgium." He used a similar formula for Holland. For Luxembourg he had recourse to an even more attenuated expression: *a people which finds itself involved in the torment of war.* The telegrams clearly show that Pius XII did not choose silence; but they do raise the question of the pope's "prudence," or rather, of the nature of this prudence.

The Italian reaction was immediate and strong. Alfieri, the Italian ambassador, communicated an immediate protest and was received in audience by the pope. Montini refers to the conversation between the pontiff and the ambassador as dramatic and pointed. "The ambassador made it clear that these messages caused strong displeasure to the head of the Italian government who saw therein an action against his policy . . . the ambassador spoke of the state of high tension and nervousness reigning in fascist circles and he did not even exclude the possibility that something serious might result. The Holy Father remained tranquil and serene, pointing out that he had no fear of ending up, should it come to that, in a concentration camp or in enemy hands. 'We were not afraid,' added the pope, 'of the guns pointed at us before, and we will be even less afraid on another occasion. There are times when the pope cannot be silent.' His Holiness then went on in this vein, . . . reminding him that God would subject the pope to the most rigorous judgment if he did not react against evil and if he failed to do what he believed to be his duty. In the present situation, how could the pope allow himself to be guilty of such a serious omission?"

Pius XII's line after these strong and noble words becomes more clear. His omissions are omissions not in conscience, but in the framework of political tradition; Not moral omissions, but omissions in the flexible scheme of "seeking neither the useless nor the impossible." This line was finally to emerge in the days following the telegrams, when calls and requests for a more decided intervention by the pope began to pour in. Pius XII found himself facing the very accusations which *The Deputy* was to make years after his death. On February 13, the French ambassador returned to the Vatican and repeated his request for a condemnation of Nazism, saying (as Tardini's notes tell us) that "it is one thing to express sympathy for the suffering, and quite another to condemn the crime committed." He faced those accusations again on May 14, when the French government insisted again on an "explicit and formal condemnation of German aggression." And again on May 15, when Valeri, the nuncio in Paris, wrote that "the ambassador of the United States asks that the Holy Father threaten Mr. Mussolini with excommunication" and that "the French Senatorial Commission for Foreign Affairs asks if the moment has not come to excommunicate Mr. Hitler." But the responses of the nuncio to Paris make clear what the Vatican line really was, and the talk between Valeri and the American ambassador was strained to the breaking point. "At a certain point," writes the nuncio, "recalling certain statements which the ambassador had made to me before the outbreak of this war, I could not refrain from telling him how unfortunate it was that no one had foreseen what a mass of barbaric force would be released on Europe. Perhaps also because of this veiled allusion, he sprang to his feet before the conversation was finished, declaring that he had a higher idea of the Holy Father and acting as if he were going to leave. But then he calmed down and became more affable again." Valeri then explained to the affable ambassador that to demand an excommunication meant "to ask for an impossibility, even apart from the fact that for several centuries it had been made an object of ridicule by modern progress, but also because its effect would be doubtful." In the meanwhile, "we should apply other means and not seek the useless and the impossible. On the other hand, it was an excellent idea for South American statesmen to use their influence in inclining Mr. Roosevelt toward a decisive support of the Allies."

The supplication made in those same days by Cardinal Suhard received the same answer. The pope had decided "not to seek the useless and the impossible." He assumed that position for many reasons. Above all, because Halifax has let him know that "England is disposed to discuss peace terms." Secondly, because in July it still seemed possible to negotiate a peace and it was clear that, if a peace should be concluded by international agreement, the Vatican would find itself isolated and exposed to Nazi and Fascist ire. Also, there were historical conditions that prevented Pius XII from becoming a Benedict XV and from making a more definitive condemnation of the "needless bloodbath." The Italy of 1940 was not the democratic country it had been in 1914. In the arsenal of Fascism were blackmail, threats, and physical violence; toward the end of May the carriers of the *Osservatore Romano* were assaulted physically, visiting Fascism's vengeance not only upon the accused but also upon those indirectly related to them. The dictatorship left to Pius XII—who was not the author, but merely the inheritor of this situation—no alternative other than that of the "useful and the possible." Still, though such a posture may explain his actions, it does not justify them. Pius XII accepted his fate. He would not be a "silent pope" in time of war. He would be a pope of tradition, in a world that asked for more than that because the Nazi horror did not fit into that tradition. And it is here that the philosophical and moral problem of his "prudence" opens up. The problem also gives rise to a series of questions involving not so much the pope as the age which, immersed in both Hitler's and Stalin's horrors and prostrate before Fascist intimidation, makes protagonists of everyone whether democrat or Jesuit, Communist or anti-

Communist, Catholic or non-Catholic. It is a problem which still exists.

The curators of Vatican documentation themselves acknowledge that Pius XII never waged a solemn and total "crusade." Thus, as we leaf through these secret papers we spontaneously seek an answer to a basic question: Why did Pius XII, who was so resolute in excommunicating Communists, refrain from launching an anti-Nazi crusade? What were the pope's feelings toward the Germans? These two questions are of great moral importance, and the scholars who compiled this collection of documents formulate them both straightforwardly. The various possible explanations (historical conditions, intimidation, fear of reprisals) may illustrate Pius' "prudence" but they cannot justify his ethical inconsistency as regards the issue of a "crusade." The editors of the Vatican archives publication point out that the hope of finding a more viable path toward peace unquestionably led Pius XII to reject that alternative. "But there is no private diary," they add, "no personal observation which would permit us to follow in detail the thought of Pius XII. Hence, one must be extremely hesitant before claiming knowledge of the private thoughts of Pius XII."

This, however, is not enough. It may not be just to judge this posture of prudence, but the questions still remain unanswered. Pius XII appears to have been a pope torn and divided between the moral condemnation of Nazism and the desire to work out an advantageous policy for Catholicism in Germany and German-controlled territories. Simplifying it still more, he appears forced into a compromise between two irreconcilable interests: "moral interest," which inclines him to side against Nazism; and "interests of state" (obviously a state like the Holy See), which commit him to caring for German Catholics, to seeking an improvement of Church-state relations in Germany, and to saving the bishoprics and nunciatures in occupied territories.

Even if we prefer to be cautious concerning the private thoughts of Pope Pius, his attitude toward Hitler in 1939 and 1940 cannot be considered ambiguous. In receiving the credentials of Ambassador Alfieri in December, 1939, he definitely spoke openly of certain ideologies that "humanize the divine and divinize the human," and alluding clearly to National Socialism, he said that "these errors, like all error, have their times of ascendency and their times of decline, their zenith and their sunset, if not their precipitous fall." At this very time the Church and Nazism were at sword's point in Germany. Since October, 1939, there had been numerous arrests of German priests for combating the "Himmler Circular" which propagandized unmarried motherhood. The ambassador of the Reich to the Holy See, we learn from a note of Maglione, "has not presented himself for months." In practice, relations between the Vatican and Berlin were frequently at the breaking point. One naturally wonders why the pope's moral convictions were not translated into a leadership detached from considerations of opportunity and expediency. The truth is to be found in the pope's dealings with the Germans. There are two key points in those dealings. The first consists in the disconcerting audience granted by Pius XII to Ribbentrop on March 11, 1940. The second is a handwritten note found among Pius XII's papers.

All polemics about the philo-German feelings of Pius XII center around the audience with Ribbentrop, and so it will be worth while to reproduce here the documents almost in their entirety so that the reader may make an objective judgment. On March 9, Tardini wrote: "Von Ribbentrop will visit the Holy Father on Monday, March 11. The audience has been secretly planned for some time, through the Prince of Assia, I believe, and through X. . . . The German ambassador has said that it is nothing more than a courtesy visit, without any special significance, but with all due ceremony. The Holy Father is very apprehensive. He does not hope for much from this visit." On March 11, Tardini described the audience in the following terms: "I entered the Holy Father's presence a few minutes after von Ribbentrop had left. He described von Ribbentrop as a man who turns red when he becomes excited. Ribbentrop said that he and the Führer are enemies not of the Church but of the political Catholicism of the clergy. The Holy Father reminded him that the German clergy has always been patriotic. Von Ribbentrop observed that Pope Pius XI had spoken too strongly against Germany. His Holiness pointed out that he spoke good and kind words in an address to German pilgrims. 'This,' observed Ribbentrop, 'was noted with pleasure in Germany.' The pope replied that pilgrims no longer come from Germany. His Holiness also recalled how in his encyclical he took care not to offend Germany even though he was bound—by reason of his mission—to speak the truth. He added that the small nation alluded to in his Christmas Message was Finland (in Germany they had said it was Poland). Raising his voice, Ribbentrop said that Germany would win the war before the end of 1940. The Holy Father pointed out that, even without discussing the intentions of Hitler and von Ribbentrop, the facts indicated that in Germany war is being waged on the Church, and he cited a number of such facts. Ribbentrop hemmed and hawed a little, then replied that National Socialism has not inflicted such serious harm on the Church as other revolutions had done. To this the pope replied that in truth it has inflicted much hardship and he resumed citing examples. Von Ribbentrop said that National Socialism had stopped the triumph of Communism in the 1930's. His Holiness noted that no one can know for certain how history would have developed without National Socialism. Then His Holiness asked if Germany had nothing to fear from its pact with Communism. Ribbentrop said it did not, for the pact was only exterior and for the purposes of the war. . . . The audience lasted from 11:00 to 12:10. The pope says that it transpired in a cordial and dignified manner. Ribbentrop left with an air of satisfaction. We hope that this visit is not exploited by German bad will. Ribbentrop said he could say that the pope still has his heart in Germany and has a profound desire to reach a sound and lasting understanding with Hitler concerning the religious situation in Germany."

Obviously this recounting of a conversation between a pope and a man who would later be judged among the great criminals of history is full of lacunae. It is taken up almost exclusively with able diplomatic fencing. Pius XII is firm only on the rights of the Church in Germany. Neither the pope's skepticism with "he hopes for very little from this visit," nor his "being apprehensive" at having to receive such a man are enough to explain his conduct. One wonders what led Pius XII to an action which, as is clear from the documents, he himself regards as dangerous, for he hastened to submit to Ribbentrop "a summary of the conversation in order to stop the Germans from exploiting the audience and in order one day to publish proof of having so acted in fulfillment of his apostolic duty."

The Vatican Archives afford a veritable revelation on the circumstances of this visit. They register the discovery of a handwritten note of Pius XII from the period of the Ribbentrop audience. This note clearly and authoritatively confirms something that was published in the *Osservatore Romano* in 1946. The note also contains proof that Pius XII took refuge in diplomatic swordplay and did not launch crusades, that he even accepted the detriment occasioned by certain public encounters because, at the time that he and Ribbentrop were discussing the solution of Church-state relations in Germany, he was in contact with German political and military groups which were planning to overthrow Hitler. The typewritten text, with corrections by the pope's hand, is as follows: "At the request of important political and military circles in Germany, the Holy Father at that time agreed to transmit certain questions addressed by these circles to the other belligerent party on the aims of the war and on the conditions of peace and to transmit the answers which that party might make to those questions. The Holy Father made use exclusively of the ordinary official channels for this transmittal. The activity of His Holiness was restricted to this alone. He presented no peace proposal of his own. Likewise, there was never any question of resolving the problems of eastern Europe unilaterally to the advantage of Germany nor of making Goebbels Führer after the fall of Hitler and Ribbentrop. The aim of the interested German circles was to free Germany from National Socialism. The attempt at a coup took place between the end of 1939 and the beginning of 1940. . . ." And the curators of the Vatican collection comment: "These sentences constitute a refutation of the Communist thesis and are at the same time a revelation. They reveal the secret relations between Pius XII and the German adversaries of the Hitler regime . . . he was perfectly aware of how the Nazi regime constituted an obstacle to peace. But he hoped that Germany itself would succeed in triumphing over its own regime. Thus, Pius XII never reached the point of proclaiming the crusade against Nazism. He was convinced that, if he gave satisfaction to those who were insisting on solemn condemnations of Hitler and Nazism, he would exasperate the passions and needlessly increase the suffering of many, and would make his ministry impossible."

This personal note and this commentary raise a number of questions. They end our representation of the true deputy, and a number of possible judgments seem to be possible. Pius XII is revealed as a pope who, even while receiving Ribbentrop, was maintaining secret relations with anti-Nazi military leaders. He comes out as a pope far removed from the accusation of philo-Nazism, and his anti-Nazi contacts throw much light on certain of his omissions and diplomatic parries. Still, though this alleviates and even refutes much of the slander cast on Pius XII, the problem of his "prudence" remains unsolved. Many Catholics, even priests, try to explain it away in terms of a "trial of conscience" on the part of the pope. But this is too convenient. Some say he experienced only a "diplomatic torment" rather than an "evangelical gospel torment," but this overlooks the fact that a pope is the exponent of a Church and an ideology in the formation of which all Catholics take part. The real drama of *The Deputy* consists in the high moral authority of a pope so bound by traditional methods that his Church becomes a go-between between states and is involved in complex and intricate political operations touching on conspiracy. Even if we do not insist on martyrdom, even if we accept the idea that a moral leader should keep within the limits of the useful and the possible, the whole point is that Pius XII was fighting for peace, which is a traditional

Vatican activity. He fought with the techniques of diplomacy. He reacted to the war and to Nazism in conformity with the principles of Catholic policy. This would have been valid in the times of national wars, but it now becomes a drama (not so much personally as collectively) because of the concomitant crisis into which the outbreak of international wars had driven Catholic policy. We must conclude that Pius was a man of his time, who is being judged by another time. The famous formula of Marx, so often cited by Maritain, on the relations between politics and religion, seems to apply perfectly to Pius XII: "Men make their history, but they do not make it freely, because the tradition of dead generations weighs like a nightmare on the brain of the living." But if certain traditions weighed like a nightmare on the brain of one pope, how much more is it apt to weigh on those who succeed him? How far will the political ideology of the Secretariat of State be able to go in coping with tomorrow's world?

We have already touched on the question of political ideology. Certain Vatican problems, however, keep turning up in different forms and require variations of the same solution. In that respect, politics is not the relation between Church and state which we described earlier; it is now the relation between Church and regime. Behind it is always the same drama: the Church's commitment to a policy of flexibility and adaptation to reality, and to remaining on the sidelines of history as the uncommitted Christian message. The difference in this case is that the Vatican reflectors no longer illuminate diplomatic or concordat reasoning, but instead cast an all-revealing light on the ideological content of such reasoning. The problem of *The Deputy* definitely involves the question of the Church's neutralism toward regimes, if not toward states. And this fits in with what we have already said. Here again, history plays an important part. Here again, everything turns on the loss of medieval power, the support of monarchies regarded as the perfect form of the state (in the wake of St. Thomas), and the crisis of temporal power that leads to the weak Church, the neutral Church, to prudence and silence as the alternative to superiority on the battlefield. Pius VII was the last pope "who did not keep silent"; and he was imprisoned by Napoleon.

Neutrality toward regimes, however, goes by the name of "indifferentism."[6] It not only has passive origins, but is built upon the positive premise that no regime can be so perfect as to merit the approval of the Church of Rome. The Leonine rationale of this indifference is well known. "The political form of government," wrote Leo XIII, "never guarantees as such the attainment of the common good." But even John XXIII, so much inclined toward democracy, frequently pointed out how difficult it is for the Church to favor one political system over another, because of the undying Catholic ideal of the *res publica Christiana*—the universal Christian republic. Even scholars like Lewy find that a Church endorsement of regimes is absurd. Flexibility, disengagement, non-commitment do not necessarily mean ambiguity, and they can be a profound moral necessity. Nevertheless, for all its immense value, this spiritual neutrality was often lacking as an ideological element of Church diplomacy in the past. Often, it was regarded only as a "free area" left to the discretion of the Vatican's expansion policy. Often, it was compromised by self-serving commitments toward monarchies or rightist dictatorships. Not that such compromises eliminated the "free area"; on the contrary, the ideology of indifference always remained a cornerstone, and only contributed to the elaboration of diplomatic caution before the appeal of "crusades." But the ideological wars have put this policy to a profound test, and neutrality toward certain regimes today may be straining the policy beyond its moral limits.

The question of working out a different political ideology is very complex, and today the problem is certainly overworked by conservative elements which seek in Catholicism a "guide to action" to match that exercised by Marxism as a philosophy of action. On the other hand, the problem is also amplified by the "progressive" approach, which overlooks the differences between moral leadership and a guide to action. But the situation is not essentially static. The past teaches us that many things can change, and we can assume that a change is possible here also. Catholic political ideology has come a long way. It has touched at the ports of theocracy, Counter Reformation, national Churches, and caesaropapism, and had a love affair with the concept of monarchy before landing on the beach of Leonine indifferentism. Thus, an abandonment of this indifference is accompanied by a search for sure ground, a political model to be recommended to the Christian. Even in 1944, among the ruins of war, Pius XII abandoned the line of neutrality toward the dictatorships and recognized that a democratic form of government is regarded today as a postulate of reason. Then we come to John XXIII's *Pacem in Terris*, which, though not repudiating the Church's neutrality toward the right of men to choose those who govern them, proclaimed the sovereignty of law and of the democratic constitutional principle. These positions, however, are not to be interpreted as an alliance with the Western democracies; they are only an attempt to fix the limits of Catholic neutralism and to establish it at least within the charter of the rights of man. The search for a "moral dimension in diplomacy," and hence for a unity between ethics and action in the political area, comes through in all these repudiations of neutralism. Being deprived of political power, it is much easier for the Church to adapt itself to history than to guide and make history. But this necessarily implies a new political ideology, one which will make moral leadership its primary objective.

The problem of how an organized religion should provide genuine leadership for the conscience of humanity without reference to political expediency seems to fit in with what the Secretariat of State has been saying. The council decisions on religious liberty, which are based on the refusal to consider political power as an instrument of religious action, definitely limit the applications of the old principles. Although there are no easy solutions, the very fact of publishing documents and rethinking recent methods (and errors) is evidently one way of escaping from confinement in the margins of history and of abandoning the myth of flexibility-at-all-costs; it is one way of finding out if it is possible for the Church to guide history instead of adapting to it. "It is not possible," wrote Karl Jaspers, "to keep circling around history. At some point, one must cross it." Naturally, it is not a question of waiting for an existentialist Catholicism. But opening the archives, stepping out to meet problems head-on while they are still topical, abandoning the habits of a Church that "thinks for the centuries," and revealing secret papers which shatter the myth of a Secretariat that "never makes compromises"—all of this indicates the will to reflect and cross over into more recent history and to learn from that history clear lessons for the future.

CHAPTER X

The Old Curia, Young Curia: Roberti

Pope, Secretariat of State, Curia. We have come to the last of the three worlds of the Vatican. These three worlds, of course, are indivisible. We have taken them separately only because they reflect different aspects of the changes the Vatican is experiencing. But now that we have come to the Curia, we have come full circle, and the three resume their unity. The Curia permits us to survey the whole broad panorama again, for the entire gamut of great religious problems is mirrored here and is subjected again to a final and more definitive "check." Yesterday's world found its exact reflection in the Curia. Its ministers never failed to express the ideology of the pre-conciliar positions. The question now is whether a new Catholic world is beginning to find its way into the Curia, or if reality there is lagging behind the ideas.

The Curia's primary problem is that of reform. The council discussed this problem as a follow-up to various accusations levied against "Roman" Catholicism, and the curial organization was indicted as responsible for the famous "Seven Plagues": superstition, autocracy and legalism, spirit of censure, conformism, scholasticism, illiberalism, and blindness toward contemporary problems.[1] The effect of the three-year run of the council—during which time Catholic teaching embraced the new positions and Vatican reality appeared more complex than a simple matter of black and white—has been to subject the Curia and its cardinals to the ordeal of a reorganization. At the same time, the Curia is being updated and its work reapportioned by the addition of new bureaus. We should, therefore, consider these two processes separately so as to understand how the problem has been faced and solved at least partially. This was accomplished more by surmounting tradition than by breaking with it. The record of a conversation, and several considerations, may give us some insight into the meaning of that solution.

I spent an entire morning in the drawing room of Cardinal Roberti,[2] an authority on constitutions and the prelate in charge of curial reform. The cardinal, a small, rotund man with the air of calm detachment that one expects of an eminent jurist, proceeded to clarify for me the meaning of the reform of the Curia. "It is a question of giving a new constitution to the Curia," he said, "since that of Pius X has proved to be inadequate to our new tasks." Smiling now, he went on: "The problem is not to bemoan what has been, but to find ways of doing better by reorganizing the Curia and the Secretariat of State. Also, there is the problem of adding new organisms to take care of situations that are peculiar to our time. For instance, many decisions which have hitherto been exclusively the business of Rome will now be made by the bishops; obviously, this will call for a certain decentralization. We may even try putting some of the diocesan bishops in the Curia. Of course, in that case the same thing may happen with them as happened with the cardinals. You know that all the cardinals are, by right, members of the Curia; since many of them have their own dioceses, however, and do not live in Rome, most of the decisions are inevitably made by the cardinals who work full-time in the Curia. That, obviously, puts the nonresident cardinals at a disadvantage, and there is always the danger that the same thing will happen to curial bishops."

Serene, but nonetheless professionally skeptical, the reformer-cardinal went on in this vein. At one point, he gave me a glimpse of what the essential points of the reform will be. He listed the changes of method in Holy Office procedures (e.g. the right of the accused to a defense), the necessity for the collaboration of the laity, the simplification of the norms to be followed in practice, the reorganization of the congregations (to bring all marriage questions back to one congregation), the establishment of an age at which retirement would be mandatory, and the concept of certain mandates being only temporary. Roberti alluded to even more significant innovations—e.g., since the pope does not have a cabinet of ministers, it seems that "mixed plenary meetings" of the cardinals who head all the executive departments will be instituted. Differing from those which are already held on occasion, these meetings will be set up on the model of a council of ministers.

Without getting involved in technical details, the new situation can be summarized in two points. First, in the future, Catholic power will be more decentralized in favor of the bishops. Second, there will be no great modifications in the remaining power of the curial cardinals. The powers exercised in Rome will remain centralistic and authoritarian. The curial cardinals will continue to be the true stable component at the top level in the Curia. The episcopate may introduce its own representatives into the congregations. The proportion of foreign heads of ministries as against Italians will change. But the reform appears to be more a restructuring than a creation of new and decentralized powers. The curial cardinals, whether foreigners or Italians, assisted or not by commissions of bishops, will still form the executive apparatus which is "reforming itself."

Once we analyze the structures of Vatican power, a real "crisis" of the cardinals of the Curia does not seem possible. The world of the Vatican government is built upon a mechanism which inevitably leads to the personal power of the cardinals. The secret of Vatican efficiency lies in maintaining the most closely knit bureaucracy in the world within a system of "communicating powers" entrusted to the curial cardinals. The result is that the Secretariat of State and the Curia (in other words, all the congregations) function with something less than five hundred persons. This figure is astonishing when one considers the immense sphere of interests that these five hundred persons govern. Such bureaucratic trimness is made possible only by the exercise of great personal power by the department heads—a phenomenon favored and perpetuated by the system itself. We must remember that, on paper, every Vatican congregation is headed by a cardinal who presides over a variable board of Italian or other cardinals. In practice, only the cardinals residing in Rome participate in the life of the executive apparatus—in the future there will be Chinese and Africans involved—and it is the curial cardinals who wield the power. The new episcopal autonomies may rectify this situation, but Roman "centralism" and "authoritarianism" will probably always recur. Future progressive elements in the Curia will inevitably tend to centralize just as much as the conservatives of today. Thinking about these problems causes one to make certain reflections on the Roman Curia and the question of its "schismatic" role in Church history. Many have of course noted how the curial currents in the council always constituted the most inflexible minority against all change. Many have judged this opposition to be a rebellion against the general will and against the pope himself. Hence, today, the common definition of the Curia's Romanism and conservatism appears "schismatic." But perhaps one should take a less naïve view. It is true that the minority position in Catholicism today is located on the ideological right, but there is a difference between the protests of the periphery and the resistance registered by the Curia in the council. The Curia inevitably plays a "schismatic" role in the Church, one of opposition to the peripheral majorities. In the Church, experiences and innovations come from the periphery, and theory from the center. It is the center too which condemns religious movements and then reassimilates them in other forms. Once accepted as official doctrine in Rome, new theologies inevitably become scholasticism in comparison to those worked out by theologians far from Rome. It is a question of a choice without alternatives. Since Rome cannot be "schismatic" with respect to itself, she will always prove schismatic toward the periphery. Rome is the apex of a theocratic, closed, pyramidal society, and it prefers remaining such. In certain historical circumstances it is unavoidable that "schism" toward the councils is instituted by the Curia. A "schismatic" Curia presents an extremely complicated problem, and it even becomes a paradox when we consider how the Curia has begun to mirror the council and its key ideas.

I have already mentioned how the most important conciliar resolutions are carried beyond the discussion stage and activated. There certainly have already been modifications in top-level power and ideas. If certain of these key ideas of the council have really become institutionalized, we will see it nowhere more clearly than in the Curia. And the reason is that certain basic ideas (the "dialoguing" Church, religious liberty, the transition from tolerance to respect, the admission that certain contemporary problems such as atheism must be met in a new way) tend to give new life to the Church; but it is a tendency which could conceivably meet with a block at the top levels. These key ideas therefore must go farther than the constitution; they must inspire more than the few spirits that gave them utterance. They must have more than a mere temporary significance. They must descend to the reality of the Roman ministries if they are going to change history.

One sees and is impressed by the daring of many new proposals. Much Catholicism is being lived as an interrogative by a few pioneering theologians and intellectuals, and while it ought to become official, it doesn't. Certain questions, seemingly bound up with disobedience (modernist or liberal), have been assimilated and carried to the center of Vatican life. However, it is practically impossible for these "ideas" to spread if they do not become institutions capable of conditioning other already existing institutions. For example, religious liberty and ecumenism inevitably lead to the renunciation of the "tolerant" dogmatic Church and to the development of the "liberal" dogmatic Church. Millennial traditions are being renounced in fidelity to new principles, while century-old attitudes have now to be replaced by new ones. Such renunciations and replacements are possible only if the liberal institutions of ecumenism are really set up and really begin their day-by-day realization of ecumenical life and policy. Hence, we ask ourselves if the shift has succeeded in giving a new face to the Curia—i.e., established a Curia capable of mirroring all the truth of the new religious trends. It is essentially a question of whether renewal goes beyond technical reforms or not, whether the council has in fact succeeded or not.

The answer is certainly positive, and it may be asserted that Paul VI's pontificate is clearly intent on insinuating the new ideas into reality. The Curia today is no longer that of Pius XII. It still resembles yesterday's Curia, with its traditional ministries, but at least one of its future dimensions is already visible, and the frequently heard accusations of curial immobility are proving, for the most part, to be unwarranted. Unquestionably, the world of the Curia tends to resist many of the council's ideas, and the men in the council who took the most tenaciously conservative positions represented the Roman Curia. Those curialist positions, however, do not characterize the physiognomy of today's Vatican. The keyboard has been enlarged, so to speak, so as to become an instrument capable of expressing a richer Catholicism.

Certainly the Curia still retains its old structure. A schematic diagram would help immensely here to give the reader a clear picture. The Curia's structure is built upon twelve "classical" ministries or congregations. It includes the courts of canon law and the various offices, and the twelve "classical ministries," which are the famous Sacred Congregations. Let us list these congregations so as to get an idea of pre-conciliar ideological positions:

The Congregation for the Doctrine of the Faith—formerly known as the Holy Office—safeguards the purity of Catholic dogma.

The Constitutional Congregation is the ministry that names and supervises the bishops of the world.

The Congregation for the Oriental Church exercises authority over the faithful of the Eastern Rites.

The Congregation of the Sacraments is concerned with legislation relative to the sacraments—hence, to marriage.

The Congregation of the Council attends to the clergy, takes care of the administration of ecclesiastical benefices, and exercises a jurisdiction in disciplinary matters relative to the Trentine reforms.

The Congregation of Religious directs itself to religious orders.

The Congregation for the Propagation of the Faith is the great ministry of missionary activity and of Catholic presence in the non-Christian world—hence, the ministry of "non-occidentalized" Catholicism.

The Congregation of Rites is in charge of the liturgy.

The Congregation of Ceremonials deals with the "forms" used in ceremonies.

The Congregation for Extraordinary Ecclesiastical Affairs is a ministry of foreign affairs aggregated to the Secretariat of State.

The Congregation of Seminaries and Universities is the ministry of education.

The Congregation of St. Peter's Basilica is the Vatican administrative center occupied with the administration and maintenance of St. Peter's Basilica.

This listing covers all the ministries, excluding only the branches of courts of justices and other offices not pertinent to our purposes.

In addition to the technical reform which is under way, new institutions are springing up around the Curia as a projection of the council's ideological positions. Today, alongside the twelve classical ministries are several "secretariats" of the council which are true ministries in embryo. For example, there is the Secretariat for Christian Unity, presently headed by Cardinal Bea, which has been given the responsibility for ecumenism and religious liberty. Cardinal König heads the new Secretariat for Non-Believers, which is an emerging ministry of the dialogue with atheists and with Marxists. Already these institutions are fully established and comparable in size to the classical congregations (Bea's secretariat has long been of such size). The council also set up various commissions and counseling bodies, which continued to exist after Vatican II closed. The first is the commission which continues to carry out the liturgical reform for which it was originally established. Indeed, from what we have said, it is clear that alongside the old Curia there already exists a young Curia.

A profusion of controversy has centered on the capacity of these new organisms to make decisions. The classical Curia functions in a tightly woven structure of power which makes of it a world into which it is obviously difficult for the new institutions to penetrate. The cardinals residing in Rome number twenty-nine, and by virtue of the system of the "communicating powers" which makes renewal very complicated, only these twenty-nine cardinals possess the real power of the congregations. It is not, as many believe, a question of complications deriving only from the presence of the power groups. A power group in the Curia is invariably the result of a governing technique. As a matter of fact, every cardinal who heads one ministry is also, because of his consequent competence, on the governing board of other ministries, to which he brings his experience and where he exercises a certain control over this ministry's activities and policies. The head of the Congregation for the Doctrine of the Faith, for example, also takes part in the deliberations of those other congregations which deal with matters touching on or influenced by dogmatic questions. The prefect, or chairman, of the Congregation of Religious also sits in the Congregation for the Oriental Church because there are religious orders in the Eastern rite. Consequently, the Curia appears as a power group within which curial politics are formed. It is inevitable that a system of "communicating powers" will result in such a phenomenon; Cardinal Cicognani, the Secretary of State, for example, sits as a congregation member in eight congregations; and Cardinals Tisserant, Aloisi Masella, and Confalonieri all sit in ten congregations. Pizzardo, Testa, and Antoniutti belong to nine; Ottaviani, Cento, and Di Jorio to eight, and Agagianian to seven. It is not necessary to continue this list in order to realize that certain of the cardinals will accumulate more curial posts than others, and that the key positions are always interlocking. Given that situation, it is obvious that an important problem is that of establishing "communicability" between the classical Curia and the new Curia which is beginning to emerge.[3]

That problem, however, appears gradually to be resolving itself. Cardinal Bea, president of the secretariat for promoting Christian unity, has a seat in the Holy Office. Cardinal König, of the Secretariat for Non-Believers, is also in the Congregation of Seminaries and in the Consistorial Congregation. Marella, in charge of relations with non-Christians (and hence, with Jews and Mohammedans), is in six classical ministries. Thus, it is clear that the old institutions and the new institutions are already beginning to overlap and that the gaps between ideas and reality are slowly closing. When, alongside the dogmatism proper to the congregation formerly known as the Holy Office, there exist "ministries" of religious liberty and the "dialogue," it can no longer be said that the Vatican world is still lagging behind the dynamic and open Catholicism of the council. Certainly, it is here that the new vistas of the great contemporary religious questions are seen most broadly, and it is here that Pope Paul's policies may be seen most clearly in operation, transforming ideas into realities. For it is in the complex workings of the various congregations and secretariats of the Curia that we are able to discern the key ideas of the council, not only alive but also being absorbed into the structure of the institutional Church.

To bring out this point more emphatically, it would be helpful to consider the four fundamental problems of which those ideas are both the cause and the effect: the de-Westernization of the Church, religious liberty, dialogue with non-Catholics, and the safeguarding of Catholic dogma. We shall therefore consider next a series of conversations with the four men who are immediately responsible for dealing with the problems: Cardinals Agagianian, Bea, König, and Ottaviani.

CHAPTER XI

The Old Curia: Ottaviani and the End of the Holy Office

My excursion inside the ideological center of the Curia begins in the Palace of the Holy Office. The Holy Office was reformed by the council and has changed its name.[1] It is now called the "Supreme Congregation for the Doctrine of the Faith." It is still the guardian of dogma, and among all the Roman congregations it is the only one that bears the title of "supreme." The pope himself presides over it as prefect, and its functions are well known: to judge and combat forces opposed to the faith and the unity of the Church; to single out schisms, heresies, and corruptions in new attitudes; to excommunicate men and prohibit books; and to watch over the doctrinal purity of the decisions made in other congregations. This congregation therefore has the character of both an ideological commission and a court of justice. The observation that a "changing Vatican" ends up finding its true focal point in the Holy Office smacks of the truth. To a great extent, what actually happens to new ideas, reforms, directions, and to the concrete authority of the new structures, will depend directly on the positions taken by the Holy Office. At any stage of their development, any of the various renewals begun may come up against a block or a bottleneck in this palace. Often, it would be enough to issue a new condemnation, or to suggest that a tendency is "suspected of error." A slight repositioning of the thousands of threads emanating from this ancient office, or a recomposition of the "structures" of this ministry, could result in the discreditation of new men and new power-ideas and in a reinterpretation of the Council's constitutions and new Church laws. The Holy Office's influence is as immeasurable as its secrecy is famous.

Old stone stairways, cloisters, and loggias—this is the world of the Holy Office, a world which lends itself easily to legend, but with difficulty to documented opinion. They all lead to Alfredo Cardinal Ottaviani, pro-prefect of the congregation and, next to the pope, the most powerful person in the Church today.[2] Cardinal Ottaviani has the reputation of being an unshakable inquisitor, a reactionary against every innovation. The cardinal, often accused of being the exploiter of an immense power and of an insensitivity to the drama of uncertainty that the innovations imply, received me in his drawing room with manners and words well able to modify this image.

Seventy-five years old and almost blind, Ottaviani struck me more as the expression of a historical drama than as the symbol of conservatism. I found the cardinal, a baker's son, utterly sincere and straightforward. He openly rejected the pathetic role of the man who looks at once both for the visitor's shadow and for a place to hide from that shadow. He laughs frequently, and permits and even encourages difficult questions. In fact, very shortly after we began talking he took on the most difficult question of all. "Shoot, shoot," he said, indulging himself in the vernacular of Rome's Trastevere district. So I shot: "Your Eminence, you realize you are considered the most obstinate conservative of the Vatican, don't you?"

Ottaviani smacked his hands on his knees with impact and uttered a typical Romanism: "Ah, no, my boy." Then he added: "That's all we'd need—for me, of all persons, to try to change everything. I was put here in the Holy Office to watch over the Church's treasure; I mean its dogmas, its doctrinal positions, those laws and articles of canon law which are comprised in Catholic truth or the means of defending this truth. I'm really the sentry guarding the gold reserve. Do you think I would be doing my duty if I deserted my post or left my position? And do you think it would be right for me, of all people, to support movements aimed at changes in the Church's principles or to favor reforms tending in the long run to give a different meaning to those principles? The Church is going through a transition. It had certain laws and certain convictions. During the 'constitutional convention' I defended those laws and convictions. Do you understand?"

Ottaviani was waiting for another question. I asked him whether, if certain laws and convictions should change beyond the measure he personally considered justifiable, he would use the same energy in defending the new laws and convictions which he clearly did not prefer. For Ottaviani not only took a stand in favor of the traditional positions; he always sharply criticized the new positions of the council, as in the case of religious liberty. To this question Ottaviani replied honestly: "Son, seventy-five years are seventy-five years. And I have spent them defending certain principles and crtain laws. If you tell the old sentry that the laws are being changed, he naturally reacts like an old sentry and will do everything to keep them from changing. But if they do change, God will no doubt give him the strength to defend the new treasure. Once the new laws become part of the Church's treasure, adding to her gold reserve, there is only one principle that counts: the Church must be served. And to serve her means to be faithful to her laws, like a blind man; like the blind man I am."

Wrapped in his red robes, his eyes straining to see me, Ottaviani spoke of his blindness not with a pathetic tone, but with full strength, with clear vitality, almost as if he were happy that his physical appearance could express a condition of the soul—that of believing without seeing or discussing. There was no rhetoric, no ambiguity here. There was a fighting obstinacy in the tone of these expressions, and a strength came through his words all the while I was with him. He spoke of the reform of the Holy Office and said in no uncertain terms: "Now it has another name, and undoubtedly its methods will change. The accused will now be accorded the privilege of a defense. But the principles can't change." For this grand antagonist of change, one notes, defense is not yet a right; it is a "privilege," and as such the implication is that it is not irrevocable. The choice of words is a logical one in this instance, for Ottaviani's personal position on the entire question of religious liberty is that that quality is conceivable only in terms of pre-conciliar "tolerance."

Bringing our talk to a close, Ottaviani took me to a window. "Down there," he said, "was the street of the inquisition. Now you can see it's a vegetable garden and a chicken yard. That's how the methods change but not the principles." His silhouette, sharp against the background of a garden whose walls remembered the ancient inquisitions, complemented perfectly the image of this ancient congregation.

The Holy Office is experiencing the period of transition more profoundly than any other part of the Vatican, and it gives us, better than any other part of the Vatican, a preview of an age when answers will be given. Ottaviani is not so much the "reactionary" he has the reputation of being as he is the Church of yesterday with its philosophical principles, its codices, its historical instruments. He is a man and an institution which clash with the spirit of Vatican II, the new institutions, the new decrees, and the new instruments. When we consider, for example, that the entire ruling class of the Church today was educated in the famous *Ius publicum ecclesiasticum* ("The Public Law of the Church") written by Ottaviani, we realize what an institution is this man. This universal seminary textbook brands as "formally unacceptable, at least in principle," any cooperation between states and heretical—i.e., non-Catholic—confessions. It teaches that Catholics must oppose, at least in principle, any state which favors Protestant schools or which allocates to Waldensians a portion of Church taxes, and that such policies may be tolerated only as "materially licit" for reasons of public order. Thus, for years Ottaviani has been establishing those "passive" attitudes toward religious liberty which have been categorically rejected in the schema on religious liberty adopted by the council. Even though principles and dogmas have been preserved, one must still recognize that certain ideological fractures *have* occurred, and that they constitute a life and death problem for Ottaviani, for the Holy Office and the codices of yesterday. It will continue to be so at least until a different Holy Office—and not merely the same Holy Office under another name—new codices, and new men create a reality completely adequate to the principles established by the council.

The transition is obviously under way. Ottaviani, who in 1953 was in Spain delivering certain discourses on the "Duties of the Catholic State toward Religion"[3] and who was making his famous conservative appeals even during the pontificate of John XXIII, has a different role under the pontificate of Paul VI. His present continued silence clearly indicates a Holy Office which has ceased to be an instrument of certain ideological currents and which has been reduced to its purely "institutional" functions. Paul VI has included the Holy Office in the reform of the Curia; it is now living the last days of its baroque existence and the first days of a new life. It has lost its old name, of course, and it has given up the Index—but it has not surrendered its power to condemn a book. For a long time, the Holy Office has avoided significant condemnations of contemporary phenomena and persons, and it "tolerates"—or provokes, it is hard to say which—reviews and historical rehabilitations of exceptional importance such as that of Galileo.

The transition is even more impressive when seen against the institutional background I have already described. Liberal cardinals, such as Bea, have been introduced into the Holy Office to restore its equilibrium, if not to give it a "liberal" bias. The presence of new institutions in the Vatican for the purpose of the dialogue with atheists, or in the interest of ecumenical activities in cooperation with heretics and "schismatics," is in fact disengaging the old ministry from the functions it performed yesterday. The prevailing ecumenical view of things does not regard Protestants and Orthodox Churches as enemies to be fought and driven out, and it implies a different attitude toward acts of disobedience, daring doctrinal proposals, excommunications without appeal, etc. If this "disengagement" from traditional functions is really taking place, as it seems to be, if we are in fact witnessing a historical transition, then we may naturally wonder what the Holy Office of tomorrow will be like. To be sure, this is an open problem even beyond these institutional "disengagements." It is a problem in that, being given a new cast and a new name, the Holy Office must come to the "defense" of a body of doctrine which, in the future, will be forced to respond to the great questions opened up by the council and the new conciliar Church structures.

It is a fact that many questions open up at the very moment that they seem to be most decisively closed. Many decisions that have been taken, leave precise ideological definitions for later. What is religious liberty? Is it nothing more than the toleration of people living religious life in a new way? Is it only a new reading of yesterday's religious life? Or is it a real recognition that all ideas contain "grains of truth"? Asserting *its* truth as the only truth, while yet admitting the right to liberty, how does the Church look on these "grains of truth"? What philosophical and juridical vision will prevail as the great conciliar revolution becomes permanent in canon law? How will tomorrow's history be lived when yesterday's historical attitudes are rejected? Today, the Holy Office is silent and is busy transforming itself. There are no answers to these questions, because the time for them has not yet really arrived. But tomorrow, the new Holy Office will have to provide answers. Thus, it bears witness to a drama of history, the drama of the new Church which rejects past attitudes and sets out to face the most tormenting questions. Behind the dogmatic Ottaviani, the famous Palace of the Holy Office appears to be brimming with interrogatives more than with certainties.

CHAPTER XII

The Old Curia: Agagianian and De-Westernization

Cardinal Gregorio Pietro Agagianian, the famous "red pope" of the old Curia, spoke to me of missionary Catholicism, of the "de-Westernization" of the Church, and of religious problems related to the end of European colonialism. Of all the concepts brought into focus by the council, by ecumenism, by the very pontificates of the last two popes, de-Westernization is probably the one which irritates conservatives most. It is commonly argued that Catholicism was born "Roman," belongs to Western culture, and is identified with the Latin world. But the necessary decisions have already been taken, and no one who knows modern religious thought is surprised by them. In 1880, three out of four Catholics in the world were Europeans. Today, Catholics in North and South America alone number 180 million, against 190 million European Catholics. Also, a new world philosophy of atheism has emerged, and theologians point out that just as "religion is a cultural fact," as Soustelle held, Europe now also counts Marxist atheism among its cultural factors. In the light of this new situation, many of yesterday's certainties are being subjected to a frank and thorough scrutiny.

Cardinal Agagianian,[1] who directs the Propaganda Fide min-

istry, is as it were the key man of the Catholic refusal to be identified solely with the West. De-Westernization would be impossible if the cardinal's missions had not paved the way for it. An
Armenian of the Caucasus, born in Akhaltsikhe (not far from
Gori, where Stalin was born), Agagianian is the undisputed
leader of non-European Catholicism. He is regarded by all as one
of the most powerful cardinals in the Curia and is invested with
autonomous powers equaled by none except the pope. He is no
longer only an authoritative "superminister of the colonies" as
one rather irreverent definition once put it. While the "empire"
of the Church is no longer regarded as centered only in Europe,
the system of national Churches continues to prevail. The "red
pope" has become the symbol not only of the Church's vast missionary organization, but of polycentrism itself. It is his task to
bridge the gap between old concepts and new concepts and to
bring about an ever more polycentric Catholicism.

My interview with Agagianian was one of the most intelligent
and clear conversations of my whole trip. Friendly, elegant, cultivated, and refined, Agagianian is commonly described as one of
the cardinals who best fits the title of "prince." But even more
than by his appearance—that of a strikingly handsome, regal,
and "Asiatic" man, so familiar to readers of magazines and the
world press in general—I was struck by his mobile, yet symbolic
language, clearly marking the intellectual who knows how to say
whatever he wishes in the simplest way. Our talk in the gold-
trimmed red office of the Propaganda Fide Palace, with its windows opening onto the Piazza d'Espagna, was interspersed with
uncomfortable expressions such as colonial crisis, Arab nationalism, apartheid, etc. I would even say that I found Agagianian to
possess what many lay conservatives lack, and that is "the layman's view of history." This prince of the Church may be a living
proof of the thesis that the crisis between the lay and the religious
cultures—a far more genuine crisis than the conservative-liberal
dilemma—can be overcome. Free of hypocrisy and sentimental
attachments to the past, Agagianian's view of the world is a
model of anticonventional realism. (Only a few English conserva-

tives could appreciate today the "logic of conservation" we ordinarily encounter in the Church of Rome.)

Agagianian began speaking with delicate irony on de-Westernization. "I know the problem," he said, "and I know that it is being debated as a modernistic madness of today's Church. But let's not forget that even in the seventeenth century, when my ministry was founded, an operation of this kind was under way. Naturally, the concept has since undergone centuries of crises. We live in history. Missions overlap with colonialism, and the expansion of the Church seemed more to serve and confirm Occidentalism than the Church's universality. But history changes. And as it changes, it sometimes seems to have a negative effect, even to bring on crises as it did in the recent years of decolonization. But look at the crisis of our day. We are rediscovering an ancient truth, as ancient as the Church is universal."

Then Agagianian came to the basic issues. I asked him to tell me about the colonial crisis, and I asked him if the "rupture" between the third world and Europe doesn't put Catholic missionary activity in a difficult position. How can the Church reject Occidentalism at the very moment when the crisis of European presence in Africa and Asia may affect the missions? How can Catholicism expand outside Europe if the accusations of colonialism apparently touch the Church itself? The cardinal answered in the following terms.

"Persecutions definitely exist," he said, "and we recall especially the Christians who have been living for decades now in extremely miserable conditions under Communist regimes. In some areas of the world missionaries are confronted with the possibility of sacrificing their lives. In the Sudan, for example, the situation can be explained in terms of the historical antipathy between the peoples of the south and the Arabs of the north—a state of affairs which has now degenerated into political struggles and even guerrilla warfare. The missionaries who saw what really happened there were expelled. Although the government which drove them out has since fallen, the situation has not cleared up and the renewed hopes of many have only met with disillusionment. Equally critical are the conditions in the Congo, although they are more complex. Unfortunately, ancient tribal rivalries have re-emerged there. Even more deplorable is the fact that this situation has been created arbitrarily as a protest against the rivalry between the great powers. Ancient unions between Africans have been endangered. It is against this background that we have to view the persecution, arrests, and condemnation of missionaries for their original nationality.

"In spite of all this," continued Agagianian, "it doesn't seem right in every respect to say that the rupture between the third world and Europe has had a harmful effect on Catholic missionary activity. Among other things, such an assertion implies an identification of Christianity with Europe. But Pius XII and John XXIII and Paul VI have all made it unmistakably clear that the Church is not to be identified with any particular culture, not even with that Western culture with which it was so intimately connected throughout so many centuries. Christianity is not Europe, and it is not the West; it addresses itself to every people of the world as a message especially formulated for each. There is no doubt that unity, understanding, and collaboration among the third world, Europe, and the West are ideals worth promoting and attaining for the good of humanity. The Church, although remaining on the spiritual level, works for these ideals. This is clearly shown in Paul VI's ardent appeal in India for a world fund to assist suffering peoples. But the Church is not bound to any geographical or political force whatever, be it the West, the East, the third world, or any other.

"The fact that most missionaries come from European countries," Agagianian added, "creates practical problems and difficulties in some countries. I am thinking especially of those countries where immigration is limited to specially trained persons. But we can overcome these difficulties when it is made clear that missionaries are themselves specialized persons at the service of the local hierarchies. Hence, it has become essential to our missionary program today to further the development of the episcopate, local clergy, and seminaries. Such a program is really the continuation of an ancient Christian activity. It is surprising how constant the Holy See has been in pointing up the need of training indigenous clergy outside Europe; it began in 1622 with the foundation of the Propaganda Fide. Later, Benedict XV dedicated a basic encyclical to the problem, and today we are reaping the fruits of that encyclical. The first Chinese and Japanese bishops and the first African bishop were consecrated by Pius XI before nationalistic movements were even born."

The cardinal then came to the subject of the political changes transpiring in mission territories and the birth of new states. He observed that the transition crisis had been preceded in some cases by violent action, but more often the crisis had been resolved in a peaceful manner. Once independence is attained, the new nations come to terms with their number-one problem which is, Agagianian believes, "that of underdevelopment." For many, "the emergence of the new nations was a surprise, but not so for the Church; she has always believed in the human dignity and intrinsic worth of all peoples. Dormant energies were discovered, and in these new situations the business of evangelization was pursued. Today, even more than before, the spreading of the Gospel is carried out by native clergy, although the task of the missionaries has not diminished. The number of non-Christians in the world exceeds two billion. In spite of the continuous increase of native priests, their number is still small and inadequate." According to Agagianian, this inadequacy justifies the coexistence of the two systems of polycentric development and the traditional methods of missionary activity.

In the realm of more general problems, Agagianian then described relations with Mohammedan countries as "characterized by a spirit of respect and understanding," indicating as an example the recently established *modus vivendi* of the Church in Tunisia, where "the Church has accepted the exodus of the French and Italians with a spirit of sacrifice because God has his times and ways." The cardinal described the picture in black Africa as "positive, although there is a dark cloud here and there," because the Africans "more or less look on the presence of the Church as

a genuine African force." Among the most interesting points for
dialogue in these areas, Agagianian places "the affirmation of the
dignity of the person and the struggle against underdevelopment" at the top of the list. In second place comes "the possibility
of staving off materialism, especially in its atheistic forms, with
the acceptance of spiritual and religious values on the part of the
new nations." Among the most difficult points Agagianian included "certain absolutistic tendencies, exaggerated nationalism,
racist conceptions of life, and of course the propaganda with
which Communism tries to spread its atheistic ideology."

The last subject Agagianian took up was that of Catholic expansion, considered not only as a relationship with areas that
need faith and hospitals, but as an encounter with different societies, different cultures, and different elites. The cardinal said:
"The missions have paved the way in the formation of new elites.
But today the problem of new cultures and new societies is posed
in terms of a re-evaluation of tradition. The young Africans or
Asiatics want to know how to take what is vital and lasting in
their tradition and give it new value in modern life. In the African cultures, for example, the spiritualistic conception of existence is a fundamental and immutable value which Christianity
perfects and restores to its pristine efficacy. But as a typical example of the difficult encounter between different elites, we have
the case of South Africa. The Church there is obligated by law
to operate some of its institutions, such as seminaries, in com-
pliance with the zoning regulations based on racial segregation.
Within the churches, however, where the segregationist law may
not enter, apartheid is not practiced. In other words the Church
attempts to make a peaceful and brotherly solution of this long
dispute seem really possible. The concept of the dignity of the
person becomes both an inspiration and a yardstick for testing
the authenticity of the new Christianity."

Concluding our talk, Agagianian traced the picture of Catholic
expansion in quantitative and then qualitative terms. Briefly, he
recalled the council's clarification of the concept of unity as meaning "not rigid uniformity, but a plurality of forms in the unity of

belief." And, with a smile, he pointed out that the ecumenical movement—particularly from the Protestant side—"was born in mission lands, out of the missions."

Perhaps the foregoing is sufficient to give an understanding of one of the most revolutionary of the concepts which have been absorbed into and "institutionalized" by Cardinal Agagianian's curial ministry. Reading between the lines of the "red pope's" conversation, one can make out the forms of de-Westernization and polycentrism taking on substance in his area of responsibility. It therefore seems to me that this interview was one of the most fundamentally important of this trip through the Vatican, for what is taking place in Agagianian's ministry is nothing less than an ideological transformation that symbolizes what is happening in the entire Curia. It may well be true that certain desirable reforms are not being carried out; but it is equally true that all that appears "intact" and "traditional" in the Curia is not really so.

CHAPTER XIII

The Young Curia: Bea and the New Frontier

We come now to the "young Curia." The Jesuit Cardinal Augustine Bea, at eighty-one years, is without doubt considered the key man of "the changing Vatican."[1] Behind all the most advanced ideological innovations (ecumenism, religious liberty, the Jewish question) he has always played a crucial role. It was Bea who first wrote the schemata for these innovations. It was Bea who rewrote them for approval in the council. The philosophy of ecumenical Catholicism and the working-out of political formulae which make such Catholicism possible can be traced directly to Bea. Thus, the ex-confessor of Pius XII has become the "hero" of the sixties. Credit for the passage of many schemata is due pre-eminently to Bea, and the modification of many schemata was often the fruit of Bea's "Jesuitism." Depending on one's point of view, Bea is regarded either as the victim or as the victor, and the most radical polemics present him either as the pope's antagonist or as his able and maneuvering confidant. But in reality the man is none of these. Head of the Secretariat for the Unity of Christians, he is responsible for the young ministry of ecumenism. And to understand the Vatican of the council, it is necessary to examine not only the men, but also their "institutional" positions.

Bea's secretariat is in the process of being born.[2] Its offices are located in one of the large ministerial palaces flanking St. Peter's Square. Juridically, it is not yet considered an organ of the Curia, although in practice it already functions as a miniature "congregation." At its inception it was given three rooms in the Oriental Congregation and has since come to occupy an entire floor. Under John XXIII it functioned as a practical ways-and-means committee. Paul VI has developed it and given it a structure comparable to that of the Curia ministries, assigning to it two new cardinals—Heenan of Westminster and Shehan of Baltimore.

Often described as the visible negation of the Holy Office (which stands on the other side of St. Peter's Square), it is an overstatement to say that Bea's secretariat is spearheading an emasculation of the Holy Office. But the fact that ecumenism has gone so far as to produce the schema on religious liberty signifies that this secretariat represents an antithesis to the Holy Office. Defended and approved by the majority and openly supported by the pope himself, the schema on religious liberty is definitely the hottest point of the "Catholic renewal." Philosophically, it is not a revolution because, as the theologians point out, it is not a matter of accepting liberal principles but a new application of the natural-law principles long upheld by the Church. The fact remains, however, that whether or not there was a philosophical jump, there was an overwhelming historical jump. Even if we say that instances of Catholic intolerance were only historical deviations from never-denied principles and from a natural law which has in Christianity its greatest advocate, it is nonetheless true that upholding religious liberty opens up the most important of the "new frontiers." Although it does not deny dogmas, the concept of religious liberty denotes living the dogmas in a different way, a different way of understanding freedom of conscience. It means attaching a new value to so "Protestant" a concept as private conscience. It means making the transition not only from intolerance to tolerance but also from tolerance to

liberty. It means new attitudes toward other religions, a new
conception of concordat politics. And it also means a new way
of running the trials of the Holy Office, a change in its provisions
against errors and those who err. My intent is not to infer a new
ideological attitude toward Protestant positions, but to review
the list of subjects which this principle raises in order to describe
the impact of this renewal.

I visited with Cardinal Bea one evening in his small and un-
imposing study (which reminded me of a country priest's rec-
tory). He gave me the impression of a man completely immersed
in the climate of the "new frontier." Slightly bent with age,
serene, in the attire of a simple priest, his eyes set deep in an
almost waxlike face, Bea did not strike me as the able Jesuit of
the usual description, as one capable only of weaving a new
casuistry. He struck me rather as profoundly aware that the
theme of religious liberty not only brings to Catholicism a pluralism of instruments, but also opens up new space wanting in margins of certainty and freighted with interrogatives—aware of the
spirit, as they say, an adventure utterly unknown until yesterday.

"The Church," Bea said from the armchair which he hardly
seemed to be touching, "is freely accepting a different set of
conditions. It is aware of the risks involved, and it knows it is
accepting a journey into new territories. Obviously, when one
sets out on such journeys there are no certainties, and anything
can happen. But isn't Christianity a constant attempt at the impossible? Isn't it a constant risk?"

Speaking slowly in the evening stillness, Bea went on in profound philosophic calm. "We are very well aware of the re-
proaches of some of our critics. We know that precisely the most
conservative of the laity, those who used to complain of the lack
of this orientation, are the most dissatisfied now that it has become a reality. We are making the transition from tolerance to
liberty, and liberty is a difficult area. But isn't it essential to
Christianity to be willing to accept the anxieties that difficult
areas bring? We should not let the progress-*versus*-reaction dilemma confuse us when we face such choices as these. They are

too big to be reduced to a question of vested interests and positions to be held or yielded. It is primarily an intellectual problem, and one which engages the personal conscience of every one of us. It is therefore natural that some consciences agree and others disagree."

As he spoke, Bea seemed to be examining his own conscience. He thought, closed his eyes, then smiled again. "No. Belief can't be imposed on anyone by law. The Church has been tied for centuries to the state, but now Providence—or if you wish, history —is granting us the gift of independence. We are alone and free, and so we choose liberty. You may say we are moving into the void. And you would be right. But isn't Christianity often a solitary journey into the void of history?"

At this point Bea paused to allow me to write down his statements. Then he continued slowly. "The schema on religious liberty is of absolutely fundamental importance. It was not mere chance that the ecumenical council of the non-Catholic Christian Churches several years ago formulated, after long deliberation, a document on the Christian experience of proselytism and religious liberty. This is in fact an essential premise for ecumenical work, because a sincere encounter between members of different Christian confessions presupposes that both parties fully respect the right of the other to pursue the truth according to the dictates of a duly formed conscience. We should never forget what Paul VI said in his statement in Bethlehem to non-Catholic Christians: 'We shall not ask for acts which are not free and without conviction. We shall wait for the happy hour.'"

We then entered into the concrete terrain of ecumenical policy which it is Bea's responsibility to develop. Many think that this policy is being allowed to stagnate now that John XXIII is no longer on the scene. But Bea himself, a man created cardinal by Pope John, smiles at this idea. He recalls his recent encounter in Geneva with the other exponents of the World Council of Churches. "I can say that this was a meeting of immense importance. In the first place, it was the outcome of a journey begun half a century ago and the goal of a series of private and confidential contacts made after the institution of our secretariat. In the second place, it was a full encounter of the Roman Catholic Church, with its half-billion members of all rites, with a council which represents decades of work in the non-Catholic ecumenical movement and which numbers two hundred member churches in both East and West. So, we must not think of this encounter as a thing of the moment. It is the prelude to the work of the mixed committee formed during this encounter to explore the possibility of dialogue between the two institutions. I have no doubt that this step will have excellent results. But such confidence does not mean I am harboring illusions. We are only at the beginning, and the real problems are still ahead of us. But it can be said that this encounter stands as a promise, as a beginning, of cooperation between these two major organisms."

Bea, motionless, seemed to be reflecting on what he had just said. Then he spoke in a confidential tone of the organization of ecumenical policy. John XXIII had originally set up his secretariat for the purpose of establishing dialogue with non-Catholic Christian religions; then he had extended the dialogue to one of the non-Christian religions, that of the Jews. In 1964, Paul VI went on to "institutionalize" the dialogue and extended it to encompass all the non-Christian religions, creating a second secretariat under the direction of Cardinal Marella.

Bea assured me that the work of these ministries will obviate the typically curial defects of centralization and forced uniformity. In view of the vast differences existing among the ecumenical situations in various countries, it will be the task of the national conferences of bishops to adapt the special measures called for. Thus, while we were talking, the "relaunching" of the bishops came up again and the interplay of new developments and events proved to be multiple and continuous.

Bea smiled when I asked him what he thought of the description of himself, now current in Germany, as the conservative-reformer cardinal. "Perhaps it is accurate," he said courteously. Nonetheless, the problem of religious liberty opens up a whole new frontier which lies outside the conservative-liberal tangle and which makes judgments on today's Vatican very difficult. Beyond the reforms and beyond conservativism, Bea represents a curial Vatican that is daring to stick its neck out. It is the Vatican of Maritain's "Christian *hazard*," and it represents an adventure of the spirit which will not be forgotten.

CHAPTER XIV

The Young Curia: König and the Dialogue with the Communists

My last visit to the "young Curia" was in the form of an interview with Cardinal Franziskus König,[1] Archbishop of Vienna, who spoke to me of the famous dialogue of the Church with atheists and Communists. We met not in the customary gilded salon of a curial palace, but in a clinic, run by German nuns, where the cardinal stays when he comes from Vienna to Rome. König of course presides over the Secretariat for Non-Believers, or the "Ministry of the Dialogue," which is the youngest of the newly formed ministries. He has as yet no house for his work, and his offices are just being organized; so we spoke surrounded by the chrome of hospital furniture, armchairs in black leather, nurses passing by the windows, the yellow trees along the Janiculum walls.

Cardinal König's new secretariat is placed at the most remote borders of the changing Vatican. Its function is the most daring activity of the new Catholicism. Such institutions must take form as best they can and must make use of what is at hand. I recall that while we were discussing the "dialogue," a child afflicted with polio was wheeled by; it was a dramatic contrast to the ushers, the baldachins, and the customary red of the curial Vatican. That contrast probably serves better than anything else to mark the birth of a new Vatican, a Vatican in the pioneer stage of working with new things, new ideas, and new men.

Dialogue—dialogue with Communists, dialogue with atheists—in general is a theme which horrifies conservatives and leads progressives to all sorts of illusions and exaggerations. Its very mention gave rise to rifts in and about the council and is apparently continuing to do so. But the very existence of a ministry for dialogue illustrates how pointless are such fears and exaggerations. It means that the Vatican does not intend to use the dialogue as a pretext for local political trading. It is not for Florence to carry on dialogues, nor for Palermo to refuse encounters. The problem has been "institutionalized." It is Rome alone that will develop the dialogue.

Cardinal Franziskus König struck me as the living rebuttal to a sophistry commonly resorted to by both Marxists and Catholics. That sophistry, in fashion today, runs as follows: first, in Italy the attempt is made to deny that dialogue is possible between Communists and Catholics. Second, as König grants his assent to Communist-Catholic meetings such as that held in Salzburg, it is deduced that the dialogue exists. The corollary is that if the dialogue exists, everybody ought to dialogue and prudence in these matters is a pure invention of Italian reactionaries. But König and the institutionalization of the dialogue indicate exactly the contrary: first, only König can dialogue in behalf of the Church. Second, since König represents the only dialogue possible, none of the other dialogues are true dialogues. The corollary of this is that prudence is not a reactionary invention but a reality of "open" Catholicism. Thus, whoever believes in the Church has to realize that the Church is represented by König and not by the Catholics of the provincial press.

But back to König. This gigantic, simple cardinal without a single red thread in his robes, without any precious stones on his archbishop's cross, with his straightforward, strong, and slightly reddish face—by which I mean a Germanic complexion—made me understand how things really stand. He lacks the reticence and the clever turns of phrase of the Italian prelates, and he speaks without fear of compromising himself, without circumspection; and he has proved himself to be the strongest figure and the least "clerical" mentality of the leaders of today's Vatican.

"Let's agree on one thing right from the beginning," he said, "let's talk without trying to outsmart each other. You are a journalist and I am a cardinal. Let's eliminate all the tactics and come right to the point. We'll clarify what the dialogue is, and then what the dialogue with the Communists is. Then we'll see what happens from there. You ask, I'll answer. This way we can begin a real dialogue on the dialogue. Otherwise, it will become a game of who is cleverer than the other fellow, whereas what we both really want is a discussion between responsible men.

"Now let's recognize," he went on, "that atheism exists; and together with atheism there exist atheists. But we don't know what values are hidden in atheism. There are certainly some positive values there, and behind the false concept that atheism has of God there are different positions and different values. Now, to begin with, a dialogue with atheism means a study of atheism. Catholics have often disposed of this problem by describing atheism as the devil. But even in those terms it's a question of knowing what that devil thinks, what we can think about what he thinks, how many devils there are, and so forth. Now if we discover that besides those things which divide us from atheists there are others which do not divide us, we will have achieved something worth-while. But the dialogue does not mean seeking an agreement or seeking points that will permit us to come to an agreement. It does not mean that we necessarily regard as valid certain positions held in common by atheists and Catholics which make alliances and *rapprochements* possible. Let's all avoid such astuteness and such tactical considerations. Let's leave all that for those who find it interesting. For us, the dialogue means study. What is contemporary atheism? How does it work? And what are its aims? And then how does it evolve, and what does it signify? For example, is it really true that atheism means cultural decadence? Or is it possible that atheism is a special form of religion? This is the dialogue.

"The secretariat does not preach crusades. It does not fight anyone. But that doesn't mean that it seeks alliances. The dialogue is study and knowledge. Study and knowledge imply understanding and respect. Hence, no fight with individuals. But understanding and respect don't mean confusion either. The purpose of the secretariat is to seek and define the limits and the scope of the dialogue. For example, it makes no contact with governments. There is no participation in the political manifestations of atheism. There is no individual initiative. Atheism often appears in an organized form, as in Germany and Holland. In such cases, we can, as an organized theistic Church, make contact with them, as an organized atheistic movement, and take part in conferences and congresses. When congresses touching on atheism take place, we can be present to explain our point of view. That of Salzburg is an example of this, and there is no need to call it anything else. An association of Christian inspiration (the Paulus Gesellschaft) sponsored a congress there to discuss the theme of 'Christianity and Marxism Today,' and Christians and Marxists attended to present their respective positions. Our presence there did not mean a recognition of values in common or dialogue as an agreement; it was rather a gesture intended to promote the study of the subject of man and religion. I mean that Salzburg was an exchange of ideas between Marxists and Christians, and not between Communists and Catholics. People can speculate all they want. And that is what it really was."

The cardinal then went on to explain very carefully that "the aim of the secretariat is therefore to become acquainted with the phenomenon of atheism, and then to keep the bishops of the Church informed on it. Atheism is moving. It changes, takes on various forms, ranging from a persecution of religion to an agnostic indifferentism. In certain Communist countries, bishops are silenced or expelled. It is essential that other bishops know why that happens, how it happens, and on what doctrinal basis it happens. So, we definitely have to foster research. It is not our purpose to take the political initiative. The secretariat is built on an international team of bishops who take part in their respective national episcopal conferences. Each fosters work-groups all over the world, since we have to deal with a universal phenomenon. Contemporary atheism is probably the number one problem of the Church today, and dialogue means that we are aware of it and that we want to investigate why man and God appear to be in competition and why precedence is given to man."

And the Communists? König smiled. "They constitute a special current of atheism, and within that current there are many undercurrents. The secretariat has already made an initial study of this problem, and I'll give you a copy."

König has a profound and extensive knowledge of eastern Europe. He has made frequent visits to Budapest and has met with Mindszenty; it is said that he took measures in 1964 for Mindszenty's liberation. "We simply have to know that world, but without the usual facile definitions," König observed. Then he spoke of certain Christian fermentations which, after decades of maturation, are now bearing fruit in the USSR, and he added: "Perhaps even the Communists will have to recognize that religion is not a superstructure but a spiritual need of man in any society." When I mentioned the fact that in Leningrad there are certain groups of young intellectuals who are rediscovering Berdyaev, his comment was serious and knowledgeable: "Yes, I know. And in other places too." König spoke in the tone of a scientist investigating a phenomenon. When he says "perhaps" or "and in other places too," it is without an overtone of satisfaction, but by way of recording an event, and he is obviously fitting what he says into the framework of the universal atheistic casuistry.

As our conversation drew to a close, König handed me the document he had mentioned earlier setting out the position of the secretariat with respect to Communistic atheism.[2] The document summarizes all the goals of modern culture reflected in atheism, ending with the recent and uncompromising positions advanced by Del Noce.[3] It is a *summa,* not of clerical, but of cultural judgments. It presents us with Catholic thought, enriched by rationalistic and liberal additions. Commenting on these conclusions, the document reports that "from the phenomenological point of view Marxist atheism is the most dangerous form of atheism that has ever appeared on the face of the earth." It reproduces passages from Marx, Engels, from the *Sovietskaya Enciclopeja*, from the publications of the University of Moscow, etc. Marxism is declared to be a "pseudo religion," with its official doctrine crystallized in positions which have not changed. However, there are "certain variations in its attitude toward religion in the Marxist atheism of Italy, France, Yugoslavia, etc." These variations contrast with Soviet positions and "tend to criticize the policy of coercion presently practiced in Socialist countries toward believers." These variations have their source in the admission that an ideological pluralism can exist in Socialist society. That is why certain Marxists today "propose and seek collaboration with Catholics and try to demonstrate that even Marxist orthodoxy admits the possibility of the coexistence of ideologies." The document concludes with this statement: "There is no question of the existence of these variations. Nonetheless, although we do not wish to call intentions into question, it is difficult to say to what extent it is a tactic to attract believers or a genuine change in the Communist attitude toward religion."

I think the significance of the dialogue is clear from the above. The ministry which, as of 1965, began to institutionalize the dialogue struck me as being analogous to a seismological laboratory which registers the vibrations, the fissures, the source points, and the fields of influence of a universal phenomenon. Similarly, König's secretariat records variations in the visible face of an equally universal phenomenon. The gathering of data takes place slowly, methodically, and critically, and calls for the exploration of a dimension other than the physical. In the light of such painstaking effort, and in the presence of as strong a personality as that of Cardinal König, one begins to sense how parochial are the alarms and excesses of conservatives and progressives. One sees that what the Church is attempting, in fact, is the diagnosis of a major problem on a world-wide scale. And, in that sense, it is irrational to expect at this time a magical formula for co-existence or "closure" with atheists, Marxists, or otherwise. Such a possibility is clearly not in the spirit of the Church's dialogue with non-believers.

CHAPTER XV

The Big Breach

I left the Vatican for the last time on a bright fall morning. Snow had glistened on the cupola of St. Peter's when I began my visit almost a year before. Now, I had the sensation of terminating rather abruptly an experience that could have gone on forever. I had established contact, in that year, with a complicated and difficult world and, as a result, had accumulated a handful of testimonies, a collection of conversations. In the normal course of practical journalism, what I should have done would be to begin again at the beginning, to re-examine themes hardly touched on yet, to analyze and delve, to survey the whole from new vantage points before attempting to draw any conclusions that might be worth passing on to the reading public. But it occurred to me that I had gone as far as one could with the method of "direct take," and that it would be better to cut off, by an act of sheer will, the exploration of a reality which could only grow in complexity as the investigation of it progressed. Similarly, I rejected the possibility of developing certain superficial impressions I had got during the course of my excursions into the Vatican. Such development, and the investigation that it would entail, would take from those impressions their immediacy and spontaneity.

I prefer, therefore, to close this account of the changing Vatican by giving only such observations and making only such remarks as seem absolutely necessary. I believe it is more honest not to attempt to draw up a balance sheet on a rare experience, to say not only what I know and understand but also what I do not know and cannot understand. I prefer, in other words, the data of experience and the limitations of reality to the presumptuousness of unverified (and unverifiable) theses.

On the day I left the Vatican, St. Peter's Square was almost empty in the December sun. The festive excitement of conciliar days was gone, and the mood of the Vatican as well as the liturgical season of Advent was one which invited one to modesty, a modesty founded upon an acknowledgment of one's limitations. The Church herself is unaware of what tomorrow will bring, consciously unaware even of the implications for the future of much that has transpired. The true significance of many things will not become clear, as Jean Guitton observes, until two or three generations have passed. I had learned, during my year of talking, observing, and studying, that degrees of change are not only unpredictable but immeasurable. A phenomenon often modifies itself while one is trying to assign limits to it; it is even changed by the measuring process itself. Hence, I was not unaware of the limitations of my chronicle of the Vatican or of its lacunae. Some of the latter are, I confess, intentional, for often I was compelled to decide in favor of an omission or at least of a certain degree of indetermination so as to avoid those errors of method which, in the final analysis, become errors of judgment. Many will judge those omissions and those variables to be merely the stock-in-trade of a journalistic account, whereas they really represent only my desire to maintain a hold on the reality that I was investigating.

Similarly, many questions are treated in their pure state in this book—i.e., as questions; the reason, of course, is that they appear only in that state in the Church of Rome. Only when an answer is given to the question of artificial birth control, for example, will one be able to judge whether it was preferable to take the traditional position with respect to that problem (changing only the men), or to take a progressive position (retaining only the principles). Today, we can say only that the Church is undergoing the torment of self-examination on exactly those points which represent the most pressing problems of the modern world. It is, in a word, the torment of the Reformation. And the issue obviously is not the problem of finding easy methods of secularization, but of finding paths which would permit such a theocentric society as the Catholic Church to move forward without being transformed into an anthropocentric society.

These lacunae, the unknown factors and variables of a historical phase, help to explain the sensation we experience when we look upon a Vatican opening itself up to allow itself to be judged on its real merits. The outward image is the same as it always was: the big cupola stands out against the Roman sky, the colonnades in a semicircle remain a symbol which resides in our memory, and the horse-drawn carriages, the pilgrims, and the priests delineate a world that seems as unchanged and immutable as St. Peter's itself. But in reflecting on this classic image one becomes aware of a gap, as it were, in what one sees. One begins to be aware that there are two Vaticans: the old Vatican has already ceased to exist, and the new Vatican has not yet really come into being.

We are in the habit of thinking of the Vatican as a closed world, rooted in Italian history and, in a sense, impervious to the events of the world; a Vatican crystallized—even architecturally —in triumphalism. But one experiences a direct physical sensation of that Vatican's transition and passing. Only in 1870, with the death of the Papal States, did the Vatican of the Baroque seem to have played itself out and an irreparable breach to have been made between the present and the past. Now, however, we are brought to the realization that the true breach has only been opened up by the Second Vatican Council. The problems of the world, in all their enormity, diversity, and simultaneity, have finally forced their way past the borders of the miniature Vatican State. The impression that one receives now is of a Vatican that is no longer "Roman," no longer a relic of the Renaissance, no longer a colorful miniature from the pages of history. It is a different image that stands out now. It is the image of a church, St. Peter's, occupying an immense, unwalled space, totally immersed in the world of today and willingly exposed to enormous centrifugal and centripetal forces.

I do not say these things as a latecomer who discovers the significance of a council whose breakthroughs are already known to everyone else. I say them to add my voice in confirmation and verification of the vastness and intensity of the breakthroughs themselves and by way of coming to the only conclusions possible. As we stand before the "changing Vatican," all sorts of preoccupations come to the surface. Indeed there are those who hold that the Vatican is changing too much, just as there are others who hold that it is changing too little. The objective process of change is one thing; the accelerations and dragging feet of those who are watching that process are another. For the observer who is standing still, the Vatican is changing too much; for the one who is running ahead, it has reverted to a state of stasis since the overtures of John XXIII. But this is not the real problem at all. The Vatican has become a new kind of camera in which, after centuries, lights and shadows and countless scenes and problems of human history, all sweeping through the conciliar breach, make their impressions on the "negative" that reflects them, not critically, but as they present themselves to the unimpassioned eye of the camera. What we now see emerging are the contours of that universal human reality, as on a photographic plate while still in the darkroom. At this stage, one can say that only the main contours are already identifiable.

The changes taking place generally follow a "logic of the Church" represented by the polarity of conservatism and reform. But such logic cannot be reduced to the usual terms (opportunism, power technique, self-preservation, etc.), for it is tied to a clearly defined anti-triumphalistic vision of history and of the Church. As an example, this logic shows us John XXIII's "overtures" as the pursuit not of a purely sentimental inclination toward harmony and respectability, but as the manifestation of a conviction that the conservation of principles can be achieved only by means of far-reaching reforms in the application of those principles. This same logic leads to Pope Paul's entirely realistic recognition that Catholicism has become a minority "in a world that is losing its faith." In all of history, only two other periods —the age of Gregory the Great and that of the Reformation— have seen Catholicism face such dramatic historical jumps. Oscillation between the two extremes of conservatism and reform, therefore, is not to be identified as the traditional swinging of the pendulum now to the side of conservation and now to that of progress. Neither is it transformism. It represents, instead, a search for a method of reform—a search being conducted while remaining faithful to fundamental principles. Thus, in making what we may call an "institutional" analysis, we find that the Church is actually pursuing its logic of conservation-with-reform in perfect balance, and not in frustration or distortion as so many have feared. The necessary reforms are taking place, and they are being institutionalized. But, as in the case of all reforms that are institutionalized, a certain essential gradualism is present. That process, so often experienced by secular states and institutions, takes on vast dimensions when it occurs in a Church backed by two thousand years of experience. It becomes increasingly clear that such a Church requires, above all, time, if it is going to modify its traditional systems without paralyzing itself completely. And gradualism signifies nothing except the fact that the necessary time is being taken. We cannot say, therefore, that gradualism is blocking the thrust of reform. De-Westernization, dialogue with atheists, and the ecumenical movement are well-delineated realities in the Vatican of today—and it is the Vatican, not of John XXIII, but of Paul VI.

However, parallel with this "logic of the Church" represented by the poles of conservation and reform and by change without compromise of principles, there are certain phenomena which indicate the advent of a new logic. A perfect example of this is to be found in the schema on religious liberty. Apart from its unchanging principles and apart from the conservation-reform dialectic, the Church is embracing new principles. This in turn considerably reduces the relative significance of the conservative pole in the dialectical process. It is a question now of what philosophy of liberty the Church will adopt when it discards the old historical positions of tolerance and intolerance, and of what philosophy of history. The council gave no answers to such questions. It showed signs only of a very confused preparation, which was a typical defect of the Johannine period, and the schema as passed in the council proves consequently to be vague. But such missing answers indicate that the Catholic Church is abandoning the traditional dialectic of the "conservative reform" and turning to face even those choices that present no margin of safety at all. Perhaps the Church's new philosophy of liberty be a "religion" of liberty in the spirit of Benedetto Croce. And perhaps its view of history be the cyclical vision of Giambattista Vico's *scienza nuova*.

These essential considerations strike me as the only real yield of my excursion through the Vatican. I think they throw some light on the figure of Paul VI, who is the truly representative personality of this historical phase. In this light, we can see that his so-called Hamletism is not the complete reality at all; or, at best, it is only a lazy man's description of a large-scale reality. The man strikes serious observers as large in scale precisely because he is succeeding in personifying effectively both of the logics that are presently existing side by side in the Church. Being gradualistic, prudent, watchful, capable of seeing both sides of the coin at once, Paul VI is a great "reformist-conservative" on the institutional level. He is courageous, modern, and "liberal," a pope who is able to make sure and trustworthy choices on the ideological plane, as he showed so clearly in the cases of religious liberty and ecumenism. But when operating in accordance with the new logic, Paul VI does not hide the drama of having to make choices for which history offers no precedent. A decision on the birth-control question can in fact mean the transition from a religion whose center is God to a Catholicism whose center is man. A decision on the ideology of "religious liberty" can mean embracing a "religion" of liberty. No pope in history has ever faced historical issues like these, issues which conceal what are in fact philosophic jumps. To ask for rapid and facile solutions camouflaged as *aggiornamenti* is simply to lack understanding of the implications of these vastly important matters.

The common notion of Paul VI as a sailor attempting to navigate without a chart, incapable of Johannine sureness, waiting to see which way the wind will blow, indicates a lack of awareness of the true situation. The fact is, it is now precisely a matter of the pope's being obliged to navigate without a chart, without stars by which to set one's course. Peter's bark is sailing uncharted waters, and there are no stars in the sky. Behind us are two thousand years of history and tradition that declare the "religion of liberty" and the "religion of belief" to be wholly irreconcilable. To achieve a synthesis of opposites, to bridge the chasm between yesterday's theocentrism and tomorrow's anthropocentrism, is not a task to which traditional methods can be applied. To respond to the expectations of a single century by means of an ecumenical council was hard enough; but to respond to questions raised by two millennia of history is proportionately more difficult.

The Vatican, therefore, while it is living a process of self-regeneration that has no precedent, is also registering the drama of its situation. The breach opened up by Vatican II remains open, and we have, as it were, a Church laid open to the world, exposed to the blows of history and the explosions of a multiplicity of problems. The Vatican is aware of those blows and of those problems. And, as Pope Paul has observed, he is "left alone to decide on an answer."

Such are the issues underlying the historical phase through which the Vatican is now passing. Behind the ecumenical movement, behind the reunion of the Churches, behind the popular front of modern Christianity, there lies another crossroad of history and Providence. It consists in the reconciliation between liberty and faith, between the two religions that humanity has longed to see live in harmony. It is the only true reconciliation, one which includes in itself all of the doubts and problems which comprise the history of man. And my excursion into the Vatican concluded with those considerations on that unconcluded Vatican which is already living those doubts and problems. Nor could I think of a more appropriate conclusion.

NOTES

1 The articles which went into the making of this book, and especially the talk with Paul VI, naturally provoked many reactions, both favorable and unfavorable, in Italian newspapers. Some claimed, without checking, that the interview with Paul VI had been prearranged by the Vatican in order to "launch" the pope's trip to the UN and that it had been accompanied by a series of political discussions with the *Corriere della Sera*. Others said that the interview "had been planned originally for *La Stampa* of Turin and for mysterious reasons was granted only at the last minute to the *Corriere della Sera*. The reactions of the Catholic newspapers was rather curious. Most of them did not even mention the interview, with the result that Italian Catholics were ignorant—for obvious competitive reasons—of the pope's words and heard them only through the *Corriere della Sera*. On the other hand, some Catholic magazines (such as *Regno*) mentioned it only to polemicize against the "false ingenuity" of the lay press. The *Regno* wrote: "It was a question of an interview true and proper, an interview which was prepared, granted, and controlled. It is therefore regrettable that Cavallari tried to claim it as his own writing, even going so far as to say he memorized the pontiff's words. This is uncalled-for false ingenuity, because the very fact of the interview constituted an event of notable

significance for Italian Catholics, a positive event. The fact that a pope granted an interview to a lay newspaper of the country where the struggle between Church and state is the most intense is a sign of the end of all clericalism, at least in Italy." They then went on to conclude that the pope had done well but that the lay interviewer was a hypocrite. Then there were indirect reactions (some obviously inspired by the Vatican conservatives) which appeared in the non-Catholic press of the right (*Specchio, Roma,* etc.). As often occurs, alongside the general silence of the Italian lay newspapers, the boycott of the Catholic newspapers, the polemic of the partisan magazines, and the reaction of the right, it turned out that only *Unità* (the organ of the Italian Communist party) and *Avanti!* (the organ of the Italian Socialist party) provided their readers with the word of the pope, commenting on it with admirable balance from the Communist or Socialist viewpoint. Even the notoriously anticlerical weekly *Espresso* quoted it, agreeing with the "apprehensive and moving realism of the pope." There was a unanimous echo in the foreign press, from *Le Figaro* to the Polish dailies. But this has no bearing on our point here.

In order to clear up this question perhaps we should explain how these articles came into being and how the interview came about. It was, of course, neither set up to "launch" the pope's trip to the UN, nor controlled, nor "instrumentalized." It came about in the following way. Upon my return from Russia in the first days of 1965, my newspaper asked me what I was planning to do, as they frequently do at the beginning of the year. I asked to do a "job" on the Vatican, in view of the Council coming to an end and in view of what it was going to mean as a whole. The *Corriere* approved my request, and so, after a short trip to Puglia, I went to Rome at the beginning of February. I let the people in the Vatican know that I intended to do a series of articles and that I was interested in doing it only by means of direct documentation. Their answer was for me to wait. Then they advised me that permission had been given (evidently by the pope). I worked all through February and March. At the end of March, I asked if the pope would consent to see me. Several days later, I received an affirmative answer. I asked if it would be an interview. The response was to the effect that popes don't give interviews, but that it would be a colloquy. The date was fixed for the fifth of April at ten thirty. At eleven thirty of the same day I had an appointment with the Secretary of State. My appointment book shows that I was scheduled for my last talk at ten o'clock with Cardinal Agagianian. This was six months before the pope's trip to New York. Unfortunately, on the evening of March 31, I fell seriously ill. An ambulance carried me to a Roman clinic where I passed some very uncertain weeks and for a while it was doubtful if I would recover. Such was the "instrumentalization" of my work and the "preparation," so-called the political discussions that accompanied it so that my talk with Paul VI would coincide with his trip to the UN. It is a pity indeed that Catholics do not know that life sometimes brings such surprises. In any case this sickness was very long, long enough to hinder me from returning to my work until September. I began again from the beginning on September 11. I saw cardinals and monsignori again and brought my inquiry up to date. Finally, on September 24, I was received by Paul VI, exactly six months later than my original appointment. As to the "false ingenuity" charge and the controls, I can say the following: I did not write a single line in the presence of the pope. No one asked to see the article I wrote on our colloquy or any of my articles. It was I who asked the Vatican to look at only the text of the sentences pronounced by the pope, and thus I was authorized by the Vatican to publish that text. The text was returned to me two days before the pope's departure for New York. It is true that I "made the interview my own," in order to assume full responsibility for it. I am sufficiently familiar with the journalistic code of honor to assume such full responsibility, a practice which can hardly be called "uncalled-for false ingenuity." If the Vatican advises me that the colloquy must be called a colloquy and not an interview (in order to avoid "precedents"), I understand and go along with it. If the Vatican agrees to read such an important text so as to give me the security of not making mistakes but doesn't formulate anything—neither my questions nor the pope's answers—in advance, I am sufficiently adult to understand what that means. It means that I have to assume the responsibility for what I write. That is precisely what I did. At this point, if the Catholics of the *Regno* are still of the opinion that this manner of doing things amounts to "uncalled-for false ingenuity," then they should direct their accusations at the journalistic profession which they claim to love but apparently do not respect. As for myself, I consider myself enough of a layman to express my esteem for a power which in our day (when the general practice is to provide the press with previously formulated and edited "statements") displayed toward me great courtesy, complete honesty, and absolutely correct methods. Bear in mind that the interview was granted without knowing how I would comment on it or in what frame I would put it in the twenty articles that were to follow it. I don't think this Vatican behavior can be construed as creating either false or ingenious situations. On the contrary, I think it shows a correct vision of journalistic honesty, liberty, and responsibility, which many in the profession obviously cannot understand. While I am on this point, I will say something more. During my illness I received gestures full of humanity from persons of the Vatican who saw my appointments for April canceled so hurriedly. When Paul VI was informed that I was bedridden, under an oxygen tent, and quite possibly destined to continue my journey to even more absolute quarters than the Vatican, he sent his physician. I say physician, not his confessor, in spite of the fact that it was an Easter morning which I will never forget because it was so painful. No one asked me if I was Catholic, Buddhist, or Hindu. Neither did I offer anyone any such information there any more than I feel I ought to offer it here. However, I am happy to make public notice to such civility, and to this gesture from a pope toward a writer who falls ill doing his "job."

2   The "Vatican secret" is a rigorous bond. It is said to cover the work of the Offices, the Secretariat, and the Curia. The obligation of "secrecy" is severe for whatever lay or priest functionaries come to know during their work. The penalties in cases of inobservance are also severe, and priests can even be suspended *a divinis*. However, many things have transformed this duty (which today displays many curious aspects, since what is printed in newspapers is not bound by secrecy) into a more or less generalized custom.

3   I am referring to an article by Carlo Bo (*Corriere della Sera,* October 15, 1965) on the lay and religious cultures between which there is a deeper rupture than that described by C. P. Snow between humanistic and scientific culture in *The Two Cultures and the Scientific Revolution* (Cambridge, England, 1959).

4   This listing of titles used in the Vatican court and offices is only a suggestion of Vatican officialdom and of the language used to de-

Notes

scribe positions and responsibilities which correspond to the organizations either of the state or of the Holy See. For a detailed study of this organization, the well-known and unforgettable *Vatican Minore* by Silvio Negro (reprinted in Vicenza in 1963) is indispensable. Also basic works on the subject are the important *Le Vatican* by Charles Pichon (Paris, 1960) and the very intelligent book by Jean Neuvecelle, *Eglise Capitale Vatican* (Paris, 1954).

CHAPTER I

1   This distinction is necessary. The state of the Vatican is a political-juridical organization endowed like all states with the two indispensable elements of territory and population. This state in turn houses the Holy See or the government of the Church. The Holy See is an entity of international law whose existence requires neither territory nor population. As a society of men professing the same faith, the Church prescinds from the state and could even prescind from the entity of international law which the Holy See is, but it can never prescind from its pontiff. The city-state of the Vatican is ruled by a pontifical commission composed of five cardinals presided over by the Secretary of State (who is, however, Secretary not of the state, but of the Holy See) and administrated by a governor. The pope (who has eight distinct titles: Bishop of Rome, Vicar of Christ, Successor of the Prince of the Apostles, Supreme Pontiff of the Universal Church, Patriarch of the West, Primate of Italy, Metropolitan Archbishop of the Roman Province) is officially the "Sovereign of the State of the Vatican." Among the offices of the governorate are the sanitary services, the direction of monuments, the gendarmerie, Radio Vaticana, etc. On the other hand, the Holy See is formed by the pontiff and his government: the Curia (which means the ministerial congregations) and the Offices (the apostolic chancery, the apostolic chamber, the apostolic dating office, the Secretariat of State, etc.). Diplomatic representations are representations of the Holy See. Also in the Holy See is the pontifical family, comprising the court, the noble guards, the secret chamberlains, etc., which is ruled by two cardinals. Finally the Holy See includes the offices and palatial administrations (the steward, chamberlain, administration of the properties of the Holy See).

2   Only the most ancient councils had the grandeur of this last and the one which preceded it. In his *History of the Popes,* von Ranke writes: "The First Vatican Council assembled 764 members from all parts of the world, more than a third of which were Italians, however. It was an assembly which clearly merited the title of ecumenical council. It makes one think of the Council which was once (in 1215) gathered from East and West around Pope Innocent III. But this time the assembly was much more representative because the Far East, Africa, and the New World had sent their prelates to it." Thus we have to go back six centuries to find councils as ecumenical as that of 1869 and this one which closed in 1965.

3   On the "progressivism" of contemporary culture I refer the reader to the interesting works of Elemire Zolla and Augusto Dal Noce because they represent a self-criticism rather than a polemic. Cf. Zolla, *L'eclissi dell'intellettuale* (Milan, 1965); Dal Noce, *L'ateismo contemporaneo* (Bologna, 1960).

4   The reform-counterreform problem has been debated at length by scholars. Many have attempted to define the Council of Trent as nothing more than a "counterrevolution" in opposition to the Protestant Reformation (for example, Martin Philippson, who wrote his well-known book, *The Religious Counterrevolution,* in 1884). But the idea of a purely "counterrevolutionary" Catholicism came to be abandoned, and one began to speak of the Counter Reformation, a term which expresses two things: the reaction to Protestantism but also a Catholic reform because (as even Philippson admits) "the fight against heresy improved the Catholic clergy, and the Church received a healthy impetus as a consequence of the Lutheran reformation." In the tracks of Protestant scholars such as Maurenbacher (who published his *Geschichte der Katholischen Reformation* in 1880), it is now the accepted norm to speak of the "Catholic Reformation" alongside the "Protestant Reformation."

5   The sentence "Modernism is a heresy, but not in everything" is contained in a letter from Monsignor Bonomelli to Cardinal Rampolla, published by Marcora in 1956 (*Studi storici in onore di Monsignor Mercati,* under the direction of the Ambrosian Library). On the complexity of the modernist phenomenon and on the ability of many

Notes

Catholics to see within modernism a clear distinction between truth and error, the reader is referred to the book by Pietro Scoppola, *Crisi modernista e rinnovamento cattolico in Italia* (Bologna, 1961).

6   The story is told that in the last days of Vatican Council II a group of "conservative" cardinals sought from Paul VI a solemn and specific condemnation of Communist and Marxist atheism. Many newspapers wrote that the pope opposed it, repeating many times: *"Jamais, jamais"* (never, never), which were the precise words the French minister, Rouher, had used in refusing to give Rome to Italy. Although it has never been verified, the story seems to be creditable.

7   The statements I am referring to are quoted from the writings of the theologian Hans Küng, of the University of Tübingen, which appeared in the *Sunday Times* (London) on December 12, 1965; and from a splendid essay by Alfonso Prandi which appeared in the review *Il Mulino* in December, 1965.

8   The accusations levied against the "council machine" were innumerable. It has been said that the work was controlled in a way which favored the curial line or that it was subjected to continuous attempts on the part of the curialists who were bent on keeping control out of progressive hands and in conservative hands. This may be true in reference to single episodes but it is exaggerated if generalized. Considered from a technical point of view, the "council machinery" of Vatican II always appeared to be practically uncontrollable because it was so confusedly constructed. It consisted of the following:

A   *Presidency* (formed by John XXIII mixing cardinals of every tendency: Tisserant, Liénart, Tappouni, Gilroy, Spellman, Frings, Ruffini, Caggiano, Wyszynski, Meyer, Alfrink, Siri).

B   *Moderators* (nominated by Paul VI: Agagianian, Lercaro, Döpfner, Suenens).

C   *Coordinating Commission* (president: Cicognani; members: Liénart, Agagianian, Spellman, Lercaro, Urbani, Confalonieri, Döpfner, Suenens, and Roberti; participating here was Monsignor Felici, who was the secretary general of the council, and other subsecretaries).

D   *General Secretariat* (Secretary General Monsignor Felici and subsecretaries Monsignors Nabaa, Morcillo, Villot, Krol, Kempf).

In view of such an organization and the names juxtaposed with one another there, it cannot be said that the "council machinery" was exposed or even easily accessible to the pressure of pontifical will or groups. There were no pontifical legates to direct it as there were in Vatican I. On the contrary, the consensus is that Vatican II was, if anything, "acephalous" because it had too many organizations regulating it and overlapping each other.

9   For the convenience of the reader it will be good to give a quick summary of the schemata passed by Vatican Council II. There were originally seventeen schemata; but one, that on matrimonial matters, was transformed into a *votum* (a document for which the thought of the council fathers was sought without reducing it to a decree or a declaration), and it was sent to the pope in that form. Naturally the summary which follows here makes no pretense to being scientific or adequate for the general public, but is only presented for purposes of orientation. For a complete study of the council the reader is referred to *La Chiesa del Concilio* (Florence, 1966), and the excellent work by Antoine Wenger: *Vatican II, chronique de la première, de la deuxième, de la troisième, et de la quatrième session* (Paris, 1964–1965).

Of the sixteen texts promulgated by the council, four are "constitutions" (documents whose doctrinal value is very high), nine are "decrees" (of more practical nature), and three are "declarations." The following is a list of the council texts with the dates they were promulgated:

Four constitutions on:

The Liturgy (December 4, 1963)

The Church (November 21, 1964)

Divine Revelation (November 18, 1965)

The Church in the Modern World (December 7, 1965)

Nine decrees on:

Social Communications Media (December 4, 1963)

Ecumenism (November 21, 1964)

The Eastern Catholic Churches (November 21, 1964)

The Pastoral Duties of Bishops (October 28, 1965)

The Renewal of Religious Life (October 28, 1965)

Seminaries (October 28, 1965)

The Lay Apostolate (November 18, 1965)

The Missionary Activity of the Church (December 7, 1965)

The Ministry and the Priestly Life (December 7, 1965)

Three declarations on:

The Church's Relations with Non-Christian Religions (October 28, 1965)

Christian Education (October 28, 1965)

Religious Liberty (December 7, 1965)

The Liturgical Reform. This constitution has already had many practical effects. In general, it defines the liturgy as "Christocentric" and divests it of other meanings, stressing above all the value of manifesting the aspect of the "Christian community." It is marked by the rendering of rituals that are directly comprehensible, the end of ritual considered as "magic," the community and assembly character of ceremonies, all of which are advanced by the extensive introduction of the vernacular in the rituals. The liturgical reform also implies a "return" to Christian purity by removing from the rituals the weight of post-Constantinian traditions which tended to deform their "community" character.

De Ecclesia. This is a fundamental dogmatic constitution which introduced important changes both in the principles and in the structures of Church power. The posture of the Church toward non-Catholics, for example, has been renewed by the fundamental concept of the recognition that "those who through no fault of their own are ignorant of the Gospel and are still seeking God, and who try with the help of grace to carry out His will which they know through the dictates of their conscience, can attain eternal salvation." *De Ecclesia* admits that for Catholics there is "a certain true union in the Holy Spirit even with those belonging to non-Catholic Christian confessions." As regards power, even though it confirms the absolute authority of the pope, *De Ecclesia* establishes that the bishops constitute a "college which possesses supreme and full power over the whole Church, although this power cannot be exercised without the agreement and consent of the Roman pontiff." Compared with Vatican I, which proclaimed the absolute authority and infallibility of the pope, *De Ecclesia* effects an integration which also recognizes the collegial powers of the bishops. Up to 1962 it was general Catholic teaching that, except in the case of an ecumenical council, the bishops had power only in their respective dioceses even in those cases where collegiality was in fact recognized in national episcopal conferences or in plurinational conferences such as that of Southeast Asia. This constitution also establishes important general principles such as the "priesthood of the faithful" (which excludes the old idea of the "flock" and implies, as we shall see below, a different role for the laity in the Church). Finally, the constitution decreed the restoration of the "diaconate" which can be conferred "even on men of mature age living in matrimony." In view of these decisions, as well as of those mentioned above, *De Ecclesia* is a sort of constitutional charter which fulfills the decisions of the council of Pius IX and brings the Church to a complete and modern definition of its own nature and character.

Divine Revelation. This second dogmatic constitution is connected with ecumenism and is an attempt to reconcile the Catholic positions (favorable to tradition) with Protestant positions (favorable to Scripture). It has managed to eradicate the prejudice that has pervaded it for four centuries. The theological discussion of the question is now open, whereas previously it was considered closed or at best a dispute left to scholars remote from "Roman" and curial theology. The usefulness of this theological discussion, which touches on the very substance of ecumenism, has at least now been registered by the council.

The Church and the Modern World. The first part of this constitution answers a number of questions. What does the Church think of the dignity of man (chapter I)? What should be recommended for the edification and betterment of modern society (chapter II)? What is the ultimate significance of human activity (chapter III)? The fourth chapter illustrates how the People of God and the human race in which this People is inserted help each other mutually, so that the Church's mission appears to be both religious and profoundly human at once. The second part studies a series of questions on the dignity of matrimony and the family, the fostering of culture, economic and social life, the life of the political community, and finally peace and war. The document takes a more or less traditional stand on some questions (its definition of war, the exclusion of divorce, etc.). But certain other questions, such as birth control, were postponed "in attendance upon a fitting response" (as Paul VI said in his address at the closing of the council). It should be noted here that no condemnation was pronounced on the modern world. Generally, considering the social questions of the contemporary world (war, atomic arms, workers' participation in the fruits of industry, Communism, etc.), this constitution chose to mildly update the traditional Catholic arguments rather than attempt a clear answer to those questions. In the final analysis, the condemnation of total war and of nuclear or atomic war which the council issued proves to be quite full of reservations and rather "traditional." On the other hand, the question of Communism is referred to the voting on atheism which takes on different meanings according to the point of view one adopts. The general lines of this schema are not "traditional." They contain a completely new view of atheism as a contemporary problem and an attempt to study it, to understand it, and to explain it. Generally, the policy of "preventive condemnation," which was typical of the past and which was exercised sweepingly, even on liberal thought in general, became, as of the promulgation of this document, a thing of the past in the full sense. As to Communistic atheism, a policy of open compromise was chosen. Even the expressions "Marxist atheism" and "Communist atheism" were avoided. Instead, the "less political" expression "systematic atheism" was preferred, saying that the Church "cannot desist from denouncing errors and actions which it has always reproved." In the notes of the document reference is made both to the encylical of Pius XII against Communism (which calls for and provides the theoretical basis for excommunication) and the encylical of John XXIII (which condemns the error but not the person erring). In other words, the council took full cognizance of the teaching of the recent popes on the question and indeed made that teaching its own. The objective observer may say that apart from possible value judgments and without inquiring whether a different position would be good or bad, no basic updatings were realized here. And this could also be said of the specifically economic and social positions where alongside the approval of political reformism and alongside the legitimation of the strike (condemned by Pius XI but then "rehabilitated" by the social encyclicals) the council document takes recourse in practice to the social teaching of the modern popes.

Such traditionalism or the registration of recent teachings also characterize the council's response to the problems of matrimony and birth control. But the council set aside for the pope both the *votum* on marital discipline (which constituted the seventeenth schema) and the decision on birth control. Let us make two observations at this point. On the matrimonial problem (divorce) the council reaffirmed the principle of the indissolubility of the marriage bond and rejected even the possibility of "little divorce" proposed by the eastern bishop Zoghby, leaving undecided the juridical casuistry which derives from it. With birth control even more doors have been left open. The council reaffirmed the principle of procreation as the principal end of matrimony. But alongside this reaffirmation, it established the new principle of "responsible procreation." On the doctrinal plane, the Church has therefore admitted that the parents are to determine "with a right Christian conscience" the number of children they shall have. But although this "repositioning" was affirmed in a solemn and conciliar way, no answer has been given to "how" this responsible procreation can be realized. Or to be more exact, the council made reference to already known positions, counseling modern man to follow the traditional posture fixed by the popes in the recent past (Pius XI and Pius XII): certain methods according to nature have received approval and backing (such as the Ogino-Knaus method) and all methods "against nature" have been excluded. As to an evaluation of new methods (the decision as to whether they are natural or against nature), the matter is left to the council commission and the judgment of the pope. On the whole, there was no formulation of the problem in the clear and sweeping terms in which Paul VI had put it in India: as a modern drama connected with overpopulation and mass education. Until decisions in these areas are forthcoming, the profound problem of "conscious procreation" will remain regulated by the nuanced and complicated casuistry of the past.

The Social Communications Media. This decree has established an updating of the media of communication between the Church and contemporary man. It raised the question of public opinion and information, in an attempt to break the tradition of secrecy, isolation, and scorn for public opinion which has weighed on the Catholic Church for so long. On the whole, however, this document has been judged by many objective observers as very weak.

Ecumenism. This decree constitutes another keystone of the new "reconciliational" positioning of the Church. It refers specifically to non-Catholic Christians and it establishes a series of extremely advanced principles. It recognizes that schisms and heresies came about, for example, "through the fault of men on both sides"; that "all non-Catholic Christians are, by virtue of baptism, in a certain real, though incomplete, communion with the Church"; and above all that to promote the unity of Christians "the Church is called by Christ to a continuous reform, excepting from this reform only whatever touches the immutable deposit of faith." This concept of permanent reform was never stated before with such daring and it assumes a truly revolutionary significance when placed next to certain recommendations which follow upon it. One such recommendation says: "Prayer in common with non-Catholic Christians is licit and even desirable, and as to the sharing of sacred things the ecclesiastical authority will establish when and to what extent it is admissible." Another recommendation welcomes "the cooperation with non-Catholics to further and enhance the dignity of the human person, peace, science, the combating of misery, hunger, and illiteracy."

The Eastern Catholic Churches. This decree signified a truly courageous rupture with old positions. It reinforces the autonomy and the prerogatives of the Eastern Catholic Churches, preserving their rites and disciplines. It also broadened the teaching which permits the communication in sacred things between Eastern Catholics and Eastern dissident (Orthodox) Christians. In this way the Eastern Catholic Churches become a "bridge" between Rome and the Eastern schismatic Christians.

The Duties of Bishops. After collegiality (in relationship to the personal power of the pope) this decree recognizes the legitimate aspiration of bishops to many decentralized powers. The episcopal conferences, for example, were defined for the first time as stable and permanent organs and expressions of collegiality. Then many powers of the Roman Curia will probably pass to the bishops because the council "expresses the desire that the Curia be given a new ordering in conformity with the necessities of the times, and that its members be to a larger extent chosen from the various regions of the Church." The council has also pronounced with this document an interesting statement regarding the relationships between the bishops and civil authority, and it may have important consequences in the Church-state question. The text says: "The Council votes that in the future no more rights and privileges in the election, nomination, or appointment to the episcopal office be granted to the civil authority and it implores those civil authorities which presently, on the grounds of previous understanding with the Holy See, enjoy such privileges to renounce them spontaneously." This should give an idea of the significance of the schema in certain countries (for example, Spain) and in certain political situations. Finally it is recommended to the bishops that they institute pastoral commissions (a sort of diocesan synod) in order better to conduct their apostolate.

The Renewal of Religious Orders. This is a rather traditional document. But it insists strongly that the religious should dedicate themselves to apostolic activity much more than in the past. It also calls for the "rigorous observance" of the vows of chastity, poverty, and obedience.

Priestly Formation. This decree refers to seminaries and hence to the problem of the education of priests. It is remarkably advanced and it calls for radical changes. For example, it recommends sacred Scripture as "the soul of all theological studies," a "solid scientific and humanistic preparation," and it calls for a revision of the study programs in the ecclesiastical universities, attributing "exceptional importance" and "universal character" to a formation with a definite "pastoral" orientation.

The Lay Apostolate. The role of the laity in the Church is of immense importance because certain doctrinal definitions can come to bear heavily even in the political relationship between Catholics and the Holy See. The council made several remarkably advanced decisions in this area. The decree says: "Laymen have the right and at times even the obligation to make their opinions known on things concerning the good of the Church." The decree also established that "pastors should recognize and foster the dignity and responsibility of laymen in the Church and they should allow laymen freedom and space for action."

The Missions. Completely transformed because it was originally judged to be too conservative, this document sets the foundation for overcoming all missionary Westernization through the collaboration with non-Catholic missions, the re-evaluation of national churches, etc.

The Priest. This decree rejected every proposal in favor of the marriage of Catholic priests and developed the concepts of ecumenism and pastorality in relationship to the mission of the priest. It proposes adaptations to modern reality, and it gives observers reason to expect a reviewing of the Catholic positions toward ex-priests and of certain civil limitations imposed on them by old concordat regulations.

Relations with Non-Christians. Apart from attentuations in certain areas, this is one of the most daring declarations of the council. It says that "the Church in no way rejects whatever is true and holy in other religions; indeed they frequently reflect a ray of that truth

which illuminates all men." Even the non-Christian religions therefore "bear witness to an answer, though perhaps an imperfect and
not entirely true answer, to the recondite enigmas of human existence." This is a return to a very old position (for example, in the
Sistine Chapel the prophets of the Bible alternate with the pagan
sibyls) to pave the way for new affirmations. Certain religious merits
are recognized in Buddhism, Hinduism, etc., and Christians are "asked
to forget past differences and hatred" toward Islam. Finally, the document closes with the absolution of the Jews with an attenuated yet
clear statement: "Even though the Hebrew authorities and their fol-
lowers were instrumental in the death of Christ, nevertheless what
was committed during His Passion cannot be imputed indiscriminately
to all the Jews then living nor to the Jews of our time." Then the
schema condemns "all discrimination and persecution perpetrated because of race, color, social condition, or religion."

Christian Education. This declaration is of immense importance for
the school question in general and because for the first time it is
said that "young boys and girls should also receive, while they are
growing up, a positive and prudent sexual education." As regards
the schools it defends "the real liberty on the part of the parents in
the choice of schools" and it regards as a "duty of the civil authorities
to see that the public subventions be granted in such a way that
the parents can choose schools for their children in full liberty according to the dictates of their conscience." The assertion is made that
"the State must abstain from every form of scholastic monopoly." The
document thus assumes politically traditional positions and makes
pedagogically new exhortations.

Religious Liberty. This final declaration is of exceptional importance
and it has a logical connection with the basic Catholic liberal position. While maintaining that truth as taught by the Catholic Church is
the only religious truth, it goes on to establish man's freedom of religion as a natural right, the state's duty to guarantee that freedom, and
to deny to the state the right of stifling that freedom. The document
states: "The civil authority must avoid all discrimination on religious
grounds. Even when there is a special civil recognition of one religious
community, the religious liberty of all citizens and all groups must be
recognized at the same time." And the consequences of such a statement for concordat politics are as evident as they are important.

Regarding the fact that the schemata of social character on the whole reached considerably less daring solutions than the other schemata, we should bear in mind several significant facts. To begin with, it turned out that the majority of the council fathers had investigated the great ecclesiological questions very deeply, and socioeconomic questions much less deeply. The French and the Germans should have been the spearheads of the debate, but they didn't challenge the conservatives on the socioeconomic issues because they were aware of not having really worked out these problems in depth. Thus the majority of the council fathers, who had nearly always been "progressive," on these issues threw their weight over to the traditional positions. If this had not occurred, mediations and compromises would have accomplished nothing. We should not forget that precisely Paul VI, when he was still cardinal, had predicted this in a famous letter to his diocese which criticized the setting certain voices were giving to the council and which set aside, as if it were only a marginal issue, the great problems of modern man. Also worth bearing in mind is the very human statement made by Lawrence, the Anglican lay observer, at a conference of Catholics. Lawrence hailed the council as a great event which has opened so many doors, making it possible for the separated religions to draw near to the Church of Rome and for the Catholic priest to go out to meet contemporary reality head on. "But the Catholic priests," Lawrence said, "live far removed from certain aspects of life. It will be very difficult for them to find new solutions to marriage questions and morals in general for the simple reason that they know so little about life." Much of the council's "traditionalism" can be explained in similar terms. Talk of an "open" Church is only three years old. Only the priests of the coming generations will live the "open" Church in reality, delving into certain burning questions raised by the council. But such typically Anglican observations should not deform our general conclusions. It is true that many social decisions of the council confirm traditional positions. But the fact of having left certain judgments for the pope means having left room for a post-conciliar "dynamic."

10　The closing of Vatican Council II was definitely too hurried. It had been prepared rapidly and unexpectedly by John XXIII and was rapidly and suddenly closed by Paul VI. And the dialogue with the world, which was clearly the thorniest issue of the whole council, was voted on in the few weeks before the closing deadline. Even the most respected commentators like Prandi (in *Il Mulino,* December, 1965), observed that "one would say that a number of questions were not sufficiently worked through and that it was hence best to put differences aside and work for unanimity by way of compromise. To be sure, the fact that four sessions succeeded in bringing some questions to full maturation leads one to think that the council is irreplacable as a forum in which the Church can examine itself. Perhaps a rendezvous ten years hence, at least in the interest of well-wishing, might well be announced at this juncture."

11   One of the best comments on the birth-control question was published by Antonio Barolini in *Mondo,* December 21, 1965: "It is a question of time and patience—they say. Something is in the works and a conclusion will be reached. Good. But then the fact of arriving, fifty years sooner or later, at a conclusion which has all the appearances of being inevitable no matter how much we procrastinate is not as unimportant as many hold it to be. In a certain sense, it is essential to the Church's commitment to the real condition and spiritual conscience of its masses, and it is essential to the expectations and evolution of human society. The longer the Church delays in coming to a modern and plausible resolution in this area, obviously the more numerous and intense will be the conflicts of those who live in the Church, and the more clearly this delay will indicate that it was a question not of ethical and truly inspired resistance, but of formal institutional resistance and traditionalistic sentimentality. Or, to put it in simple terms, that it was a question of a series of resistances very similar to those which gave rise to the countless great and small cases that find in Galileo their perennial prototype, as well as to all the other troubles related to and consequent upon these perfectly useless and contemptible diatribes. As history has demonstrated, those resistances were not based on religious values at all, but on artificial and mechanical pretexts, prejudices, and abuses of religiosity. In any case, as things stand, we know quite well from direct Catholic sources and reliable indirect sources that:

"A   the problem is being studied and piles of papers on the question are being accumulated;

"B   the matter touches on questions which are often new, delicate, and unknown, at least up to very recently, particularly to the ecclesiastical world;

"C in the final analysis, the decision is up to the pope;

"D judging from his statements before the United Nations and other recent postures assumed in this area, the pope's position is that of great reserve and reluctance and, at least for the present, basically inclined toward a reinforcement of the *status quo.*

"There is no doubt that for many believers fidelity to the Church of Rome continues to be put to a hard test. But they also know that it is their duty to use all their moral strength in fighting certain perennial forms of contamination and corruption of their substance. As the primary cause there is the perennial and ever recurring moralistic aesthetism which is so damaging to all well-constructed and organic ethics. But there are rumors of significant Catholic forces aimed at entrusting the solution to the conscience and to the responsibility of each single married couple, in other words to the only persons who can always be in a position to decide on the ethical possibility of their having or not having children. If the Church were to take this position, it is obvious that Catholic teaching in this area would take its place as the most open and unprejudiced solution and at the same time the most Christian, the solution most illuminated by charity and responsibility. And in certain aspects, it would be the solution most consistent with the sources of Christian teaching and of its original tradition. Let us hope this will prove true, because the liberty and morality that this possible new posture of the Church of Rome would pour out on the world would certainly be of enormous significance for a large part of humanity."

12 See Luigi Salvatorelli, *Sommario della storia d'Italia* (Turin, 1963), pp. 381–540.

13 The theologian Hans Küng used the expression "post-vatican Church" in the *Sunday Times* (London), December 12, 1965.

14 See Francesco Vitelleschi Nobili (Pomponio Leto), *Otto mesi a Roma durante il Concilio Vaticano. Impressioni di un contemporaneo* (Rome, 1873).

15 The freedom enjoyed by the council fathers in Vatican II can be appreciated if we reread certain pages by von Ranke on Vatican I: "Even in convoking the council, the pope firmly maintained the prin-

ciple of his primacy, excluding all free debate. This principle was asserted very clearly and strongly, and from the concept of the primacy it was deduced that the right to make proposals belonged to the pope alone. It is not that the bishops could make no proposals at all; they could make proposals, but they had first to submit them to the pope or to the congregation set up for that purpose. In the earlier Lateran Councils too there were congregations charged with examining proposals. But the latter congregations had been elected by the assembly. This time, it was the pope himself who looked to appointing those who would make up their membership . . . he excluded Curia men from them so as not to be influenced even by the Curia."

16 All the secretariats (for non-Catholics, non-Christians, and non-believers) were officially continued at the beginning of 1966 together with almost all the council commissions.

CHAPTER II

1 This translation which the pope gave to the Psalm was the occasion of an amusing episode. A collaborator of the Catholic newspaper *Avvenire d'Italia* made use of this translation in the future tense in order to poke fun at the pope's interviewer, meaning that either the pope doesn't know Latin or else the *Corriere*'s journalist doesn't know it. Naturally the newspaper of the Bologna diocese decided it was a "humanistic lacuna" on my part, obviously never imagining any other possibility. The fact is that since the pope was on the verge of his trip to the United Nations, his action was future and therefore it could have been that he was not translating, but only *referring* to the Psalm with a view to adapting it to his next sentence in Italian. Moreover, the Biblical text is originally Hebrew, and the pope could have been translating the verb in the future which the Hebrew leaves somehow up to the discretion of the reader. For Hebrew verbs have no definite tenses, but only the two "modes" of complete and incomplete action, the latter of which is never clearly past or future and is always ambiguously apt for either rendering. Furthermore, there are numerous differences among official translations of the Bible in both Latin and Italian. All this was brought to the attention of the *Avvenire d'Italia*'s merciless censor by a learned and kind lady, a certain Pro-

fessor Berther. And so the outcome was that the pope knows Latin and Hebrew, and that I am an excellent humanist. However, my humble opinion is that in discussion, the pope was not consciously choosing between the Vulgate and other translations, but was simply adapting the Psalm to his own future action. As a matter of fact, he began the whole statement in the future: "We will have to do as the Psalm says." And once he began in the future, how should he go on? In the past tense in order to please the Bologna diocesan newspaper?

2 This is from a celebrated poem by Eugenio Montale: *Ossi di Seppia* (Turin, 1942):

> talora ci si aspetta
> di scoprire uno sbaglio di Natura
> il punto morto del mondo, l'anello che non tiene
> il filo da disbrogliare che finalmente ci metta
> nel mezzo di una verità.

> Sometimes we expect to discover there
> a mistake of Nature:
> the point where the world stops, the link that doesn't hold,
> the thread to be untangled which may lead us in the end
> into the midst of a truth.

(Free translation by R.T.K.)

CHAPTER III

1 The new interior decoration of the pontifical apartment was carried out in the summer of 1964 by a Lombard painter (Bellini) while Paul VI was vacationing in Castel Gandolfo. A statue of St. Raffael of Mantegazza found in the Milan Cathedral patrimony was placed in the hall of the antechamber. A fifth-century statue of St. Ambrose was set up in the room next to that antechamber. These are "Milanese" particulars in the new Vatican. In that second room there is also a bronze figure of John XXIII by the sculptor Scorzelli. In other rooms there are a number of other modern paintings and sculpture by such artists as Manfrini, Filocamo, Bodini, and Consadori. Then there

are Italian gothic and early Renaissance masterpieces by Taddeo
Gaddi, Mino da Fiesole, and Arnolfo di Cambio.

2 Monsignor Loris Capovilla, John XXIII's private secretary, has
written me a very interesting letter in connection with the tower,
Vatican ostentation, *colbaks,* etc. He says: "The truth is that John
XXIII resumed the project begun by Pius XI, no less, when the as-
tronomical observatory was moved out to Castel Gandolfo in 1927.
Pius XI had decided to give absolute priority to the work of restoration
of the papal residence, and consequently the famous tower of Nicolas
V was threatening to fall into ruin. Pius XII in his turn suspended
the deliberations of the Pontifical Commission of the Vatican City-
state because of the war and then postwar problems. The work on
the tower was carried out, together with other urgent works, in the
years 1961–1962 under the care of the above-mentioned commission
and other responsible offices. Personally, John XXIII did not want
the complete execution of the project; he would have been content
with a little office where he could work in peace away from the noise
of St. Peter's Square." As to John XXIII's taste for ostentation, Monsignor Capovilla says that "Pope John was occupied with many other
things and decided only to initiate, unnoticed as it were, a change
which he held necessary but which he prophesied would be the work
of his successor." As to the *colbaks,* "Pius XII did not eliminate the
gendarmes in gala uniform . . . but it is true that he limited their
presence to some extent in the audiences." Thus it turns out to be
true that John XXIII had the combination office and retreat in the
tower made, and with pleasure. And he had too much to do to reduce
the ostentation so he allowed it to continue. Pius XII had eliminated
the *colbaks* to some extent in the audience rooms and . . . under
John XXIII the *colbaks* returned. Nothing very serious in all this. One
colbak more or less doesn't really change the situation. John XXIII
remains a great pope who opened the council and he probably enjoyed the gendarmes in gala uniform as well as the silence of the
broken-down tower he had rebuilt. What we end up with is that
every pope does something he takes pleasure in, but the ostentation
is never really reduced.

3 Monsignor Carlo Colombo, theologian, born in Olginate (Milan)
on April 13, 1909; named bishop of Vittoriana in 1964; president of

the Giuseppe Toniolo Institute for Christian Democratic Studies; appointed council expert by Paul VI.

4   There exists the edition of the constitution *De Ecclesia* with a preface by Monsignor Parente (Rome, 1965) who explains its binding character. This constitution is dogmatic. But it is not *de fide,* which means it can be reformed by another council. This would be impossible for certain *de fide* dogmas like papal infallibility, for example.

5   The institution of the synod was followed by a certain delusion because Paul VI postponed the first convocation until 1967. In any case, since the consultative organ was a decision of the present pope, only his successor could abolish it or reduce it to silence.

6   I am not referring to the opinions of Father Gauthier (*La Chiesa dei poveri,* Florence, 1965).

7   The parish priest Guilio Bevilacqua of the Oratory of St. Phillip in Brescia is noted for having been the "spiritual guide" of Montini as a young priest. His elevation from parish priest to cardinal occurred on February 26, 1965. He participated in the ceremony of the consistory and died shortly afterward. He was a vastly cultured man who lived among the youth of the Brescian Oratory. He had been nominated council expert and consultant in the Congregation of Religious by Paul VI.

8   The Vatican *sediari,* dressed in red, are in fact a little like the ushers of a government prefecture. They receive the visitor, hand him over to the chief stewards, and are no more numerous in the Vatican than their equivalents in any small Italian government office. You always see the same ones, of which there are about ten. When the pope goes out in the *sedia gestatoria,* it is the *sediari* who carry the *sedia* on their shoulders. They are something like house ushers who double as chauffeurs, except that the *sediari* do everything by foot. Italian millionaire families frequently have more domestics than there are *sediari* in the Vatican. These men are mere employees, and they cannot be considered the real problem of the court.

Notes

1 Cardinal Giovanni Colombo, Archbishop of Milan as of August, 1963, successor to Montini; born in Caronno (Milan) on December 6, 1902, and rector of the seminary of Venegono until his nomination to the archbishopric.

2 See Hans Küng, *The Reform of the Roman Church*, in the *Sunday Times* (London), December 12, 1965.

3 Until about the year 1000, the cardinals residing in Rome or in the suburban dioceses were only counselors and collaborators of the pope. In 1150 they formed a sacred college, and in 1179 they became the exclusive electors of the pope, and it was only in the thirteenth century that prelates residing outside Rome were also nominated cardinals. Thereupon, the cardinals began to "precede" (in the scale of hierarchical values) the bishops and archbishops, and began to be considered as princes of Vatican blood and Vatican citizens even if they did not reside in Italy. Up to the sixteenth century their number never exceeded thirty. In 1586, Sixtus V raised their number to seventy. In 1962, John XXIII established that all be honored with the episcopal dignity. In February, 1965, Paul VI increased the sacred college (which at the time had seventy-seven members) to 103 cardinals and included three patriarchs. The first Negro cardinal, Laurian Rugambwa, was created by John XXIII.

By way of mere orientation, the powers in the government of the Holy See may be outlined as follows:

Legislative Power: the pope (at all times); the bishops and cardinals (in council); and now the synod, when the pope wishes it.

Consultative Power: (a) the bishops in synod (but only when the pope wishes to convoke it); (b) in the past, the sacred college of cardinals has been a consultative organ, but it does not presently have this power.

Elective Power: the sacred college of cardinals as a "body."

Executive Power: all the cardinals are individually included by right in the congregations or ministries of the Curia, which means in the pope's executive apparatus.

CHAPTER V

1 Amleto Giovanni Cicognani was created cardinal in 1958 by John XXIII and appointed Secretary of State. He was born in Brisighella (Faenza) on February 24, 1883. He spent many years as papal nuncio in the United States under the pontificates of Pius XI and Pius XII. According to Dalla Torre (*Memorie,* Milan, 1965), it was expected that he would be elected pope in 1963 and the *Osservatore Romano* had the announcement of his election ready while the enclave was still in session.

2 The Secretariat of State was born as a bureaucratic organ of the popes "for the necessity of corresponding more frequently in careful and secret form," as the pontifical yearbook says. Thus, outside the apostolic chancery (which had been formed at the end of the fourth century out of the groups of "notaries" who took care of the preparation of pontifical documents and the archives), new organs emerged such as the secret chamber of Martin V and the apostolic secretariat organized by Innocent III, which today are part of the Secretariat of State (the Chancery of Briefs, etc.). Finally, Leo X created another office, that of the *secretarius intimus,* to assist Cardinal de Medici who assumed direction of the affairs of state. Thus initiated, the Secretariat of State then came to be directed always by the *cardinal-nephew,* which means by the pope's prime minister. When the figure of the cardinal-nephew was abolished in 1692, the *secretarius* assumed those powers, unified the two jurisdictions, and became Secretary of State. It was Pius X who divided the Secretariat in 1908 into three sections: Extraordinary Affairs, Ordinary Affairs, and Apostolic Briefs.

CHAPTER VI

1 The Extraordinary Affairs Section is truly and properly a congregation attached to the Secretariat of State, for it is a ministry directly

"subjected" to the pope by means of the Secretary of State. It was instituted by Pius VII in 1814.

2   Antonio Samoré, titular archbishop of Tirnovo, Secretary of Extraordinary Ecclesiastical Affairs and successor to Tardini in this position. He was born in Bardi (Piacenza) on December 4, 1905, and is a consultant of the Holy Office and of numerous curial "ministries."

3   On the question of Church and state I refer the reader to the most significant work by Giovanni Spadolini: *Il papato socialisto* (Milan, 1950).

4   Giovanni Spadolini, *op. cit.*, who brings out the democratic and republican origins of Christianity and shows the "reactionary" positions of Catholicism to be relatively recent historical phenomena.

5   This judgment on Pius XI was also taken from *Il papato socialisto, op. cit.*

6   Archbishop Monsignor Michele Pellegrino of Turin made the following declarations to the Turin daily, *La Stampa* (January 16, 1966): "For goodness' sake, let's be done with the idea of a Catholic state. As a bishop I would like all citizens to be good Catholics. But the state should be lay. What Cavour once said still applies today: 'a free Church in a free state.' But both should really respect the liberty of the other." These truly exemplary words by a bishop can definitely be linked together with the famous discourse delivered by Montini in the Roman City Hall just before the council, while he was still cardinal. In that speech, the present pope stressed the meaning of the Cavourian formula. "And in 1861 the voice of Cavour," said Montini, "affirmed for all of us with deep emotion and force that no other city than Rome could give to the Italian nation the fullness of its dignity as a state." But there are facts (the question of the Catholic president of Italy, a question exacerbated in truly disconcerting terms by the elections of Saragat; or the question of Vatican policy toward South America) which at least condition the assumption that the Secretariat of State is still in line with these positions.

CHAPTER VII

1   Different from the Extraordinary Affairs Section, that of the Ordinary Affairs is purely a section of the Secretariat of State. It is run
not by a "Secretary," but by the Substitute for Ordinary Affairs.

2   Angelo Dell'Acqua, titular Archbishop of Chalcedon; born in
Milan on December 9, 1903; created archbishop in 1958, and successor, in the position of Substitute, to Monsignor Montini.

CHAPTER VIII

1   The bibliography on the financial-economic question is vast. The
reader might consult the following: G. D. Tiepolo, *Le leggi ecclesi-
astiche annotate* (Turin, 1881); M. Falco, *Il riordinamento della
proprietà ecclesiastica* (Turin, 1910); Gaetano Zinali, *I rapporti finan-
ziari tra Stato e Chiesa* (Milan, 1943); Vittorio Gorresio, *L'Ottocento
scomunicato* (Florence, 1958); M. Leon Christiani, *Vatican politique*
(Paris, 1956); Luigi Salvatorelli, *La politica della Santa Sede dopo
la guerra* (Milan, 1937); Gaetano Salvemini, *Clericali e Laici* (Rome,
1958); Giovanni Grilli, *La finanza vaticana in Italia* (Rome, 1961).
For the most part these studies reflect the radical or even the Communist viewpoint. To my knowledge, there exists no Catholic study
of the question.

CHAPTER IX

1   *Le Saint Siége et la guerre en Europe* (*Actes et documents du
Saint Siége relatif à la seconde guerre mondiale,* Volume I), published
by the Secretariat of State of His Holiness, edited by Pierre Blet,
Angelo Martini, Burkhart Schneider (Vatican City, December 4,
1965). All the following quotations were taken from this volume
which contains 379 documents.

2   See Ritter, *I cospiratori of July 20, 1944. Carl Goerdeler and the*

Notes

Anti-Nazi Opposition (Turin, 1960). See also Günter Lewy, *The Catholic Church and Nazi Germany* (New York, 1964).

3 See Giuseppe Dalla Torre, *Memorie*. This man, who was for forty years head of the *Osservatore Romano,* writes: "At the death of Pius XI, Cardinal Pacelli received the personalities who came to pay their respects to the deceased pope. He was extremely courteous and solicitous with the representatives of the Italian government. He personally accompanied Galeazzo Ciano who came with an official party to pay his respects, and he also accompanied him to the door. This was only an indication of his way of thinking, which was so different from that of his predecessor. He was of the opinion that a rigorous policy was harmful, and that open negotiation would be more fruitful in overcoming the present difficulties even to the point of leading to a complete and lasting understanding and to finally rendering the conciliation effective to the advantage of the Church and of the state."

4 See Giuseppe Dalla Torre, *Memorie, op. cit.* We learn from the records of Dalla Torre that the famous exclamation of Benedict XV against the "needless bloodbath" of the great war (an exclamation which profoundly shook the world and added significantly to the image of Catholicism as an evangelical mission) would never have been made had the political-diplomatic mentality of the Secretariat of State prevailed. Dalla Torre says: "The pope wanted to have the Secretariat of State consider the document before he communicated it to its addressee. He was disposed to welcome whatever observations the Secretariat might find fitting. Monsignor Pietro Ciriaci, who is today a member of the Sacred College of Cardinals and who was then one of the most esteemed framers of documents expressing current policy, saw precisely in the words 'needless bloodbath' something capable of weakening the will to bear arms in the belligerent forces. His observation was submitted to Benedict XV together with other observations. The pope thought about it very carefully and incorporated into his statement all the observations except precisely this one which was of such decisive value and importance. He took upon himself the entire responsibility."

5 The rift between the "Ratti line" and the "Pacelli line" toward Fascism would have been deepened. The concordat and certain initial

positions cast upon Pius XI, perhaps more than was due, the shadow of friendship toward the rightist totalitarian regimes. But during and after the war with Ethiopia, relations between the Fascist regime and the Vatican became strained both as a result of the positions taken by Catholic Action and as a result of the posture of Pius XI, whose anti-Nazi encyclical was for that matter in direct contrast with the Italian-German pact. On the other hand, Pacelli came to the throne with the intention (and the illusion) of being able to heal this dissension by inaugurating the policy of negotiation.

6   See Giovanni Spadolini, *Il papato socialisto, op. cit.*

CHAPTER X

1   See Michael de la Bedoyère, *Objections to Roman Catholicism,* (London, 1964).

2   Francesco Roberti, born in Pergola on July 7, 1889, was created cardinal by John XXIII in 1958. He is Prefect of the Supreme Tribunal of the Apostolic Signature, and a member of three congregations and of the Pontifical Commission for the Revision of the Codex of Canon Law.

3   The problem of "communicating powers" is quite easy to explain. Of the 101 cardinals in the Sacred College, for example, only 28 were residing (officially) in Rome when I was writing this book. Each of these twenty-eight belonged to a congregation (or ministry) as prefect, or as secretary (in those cases where the pope is the prefect), or as a member. Being in a certain ministry results in the cardinal possessing a certain number of "competences" in other ministries, which vary according to the ministry and according to the position held in the first. In the period in which this book was written, for example, Ottaviani, the Secretary of the Holy Office, also sat in seven other ministries. Cardinal Browne, who also belongs to the Holy Office, belonged to only four other ministries. Through the position held and through the ministry which they direct, the men who occupied the most positions in 1965 by reason of the system of "communicating powers" were: Cicognani, who as Secretary of State be-

longed to eight ministries, to the finance commissions, and to the organs of the governorate; Aloisi Masella, congregation prefect, member of eight other ministries, member of the tribunal and of the finance commissions; Tisserant, congregation prefect, member of nine others, and member of the tribunal; Ottaviani, congregation prefect, and member of seven other ministries. We can make a rapid listing as follows: Cicognani, 11 positions; Aloisi Masella, 10; Ciriaci, 10; Confalonieri, 10; Tisserant, 10; Antoniutti, 9; Testa, 9; Pizzardo, 9; Ottaviani, 8; Cento, 8; Di Jorio, 8; Agagianian, 7; Ferretto, 6; Marella, 6; Bea, 5; Browne, 5; Giobbe, 5; Larraona, 5; Roberti, 5; Traglia, 5; Bacci, 4; Coppello, 4; De Costa, 4; Forni, 4; Bracci, 3; Heard, 3; Morando, 3; Albareda, 2. Even the cardinals not residing in Rome have, for the same reason, multiple mandates and corresponding positions. But, needless to say, the true Roman Curia is made up of those who reside in Rome.

The prefects or secretaries of the twelve congregations are generally very old. In 1965 these were the cardinals (with their respective ages): Agagianian (70), Aloisi Masella (86), Antoniutti (67), Ciriaci (80), Confalonieri (72), Larraona (78), Marella (70), Ottaviani (75), Pizzardo (88), Testa (79), Tisserant (81). Secretary of State Cicognani was 82, and the president of the Tribunal of the Signature, Roberti, was 76.

In the Vatican, they say there is a "Curia technique." Everything is written. The congregations are born as work groups of cardinals associated with the pope in the government. But naturally it is the prefect or secretary who really governs at the pope's side. The prefect personifies the congregation. Other cardinals have only a consultative role. It is commonly thought that whoever is in the Holy Office "dominates" by right in the other congregations. In reality one sits in the Holy Office because he is in the consistorial and not vice versa. The general directives (the "pontifical line") come from the secretariat and the Curia is all the ministries who put this line into concrete forms in the government of their respective ministries. Plenary meetings do exist but, as Tardini once said, "the plenary meetings provide the more or less enlightened opinion of the cardinals." For every act, a file is compiled on the basis of precedents. Then the prefect decides and submits the decisions to the pope in the so-called "tabella" audiences. It is established exactly how often a prefect can go to the pope. In the past, the Secretary of the Holy Office always had the greatest number of audiences.

CHAPTER XI

1   The reform of the Holy Office was made effective with the *Motu Proprio* of Paul VI dated December 6, 1965. After 427 years of history, the congregation founded by Paul III is being renewed in the following way: it is now called *Congregatio pro doctrina Fidei;* what was previously only a safekeeping and judiciary function will now tend to promote doctrinary studies and investigations; the technique of trials (so secret that it ended with the excommunication of the guilty without even hearing him) has been profoundly changed. The famous "commissary" (the investigating judge) no longer sits among the heads of the congregations; the bishops of the region where the "errors" occurred will be heard before the sentence is determined; the index of forbidden books continues, but it cannot condemn a publication before having allowed its author to state his case; trial will transpire in an ordinary way and hence will not be secret; the accused will be able to choose a defense attorney from among a body of such attorneys which is being instituted. Moreover, the ministry will now dispose of consultants chosen by the pope "all over the world from among men who are outstanding for their prudence, doctrine, and specializations."

2   Alfredo Ottaviani, born in Rome on October 29, 1890. He was created cardinal by Pius XII in 1953, is secretary of the Congregation for the Doctrine of Faith (formerly the Holy Office). He is the son of a baker in Trastevere (one of Rome's poorest sections), an ex-pupil of the Roman Seminary, and is noted for having passed his entire career in the Secretariat of State and the Curia, without ever having left Rome.

3   See *Deberes del estado catolico con la religión, discurso pronunciado por el cardenal Ottaviani en el Aula Magna del Pontificio Ateneo Lateranense de Roma* (Madrid, 1953).

Notes

1   Gregorio Pietro Agagianian, born in Akhaltsikhe on September 18, 1895, created cardinal in 1946, prefect of the Congregation of the Propagation of the Faith, ex-student of the College of the Propagation of the Faith, "discovered" by Pope Pius X, fellow-student of Spellman. After his studies in Rome, he was a parish priest in Tiflis and returned to Rome to succeed Tardini in the chair of dogmatic theology in the Missionary University. Pius XI sent him to Lebanon as apostolic visitor. Pius XII called him to the Roman Curia in 1945.

CHAPTER XIII

1   Augustine Bea, born in Riedböhringen (Freiburg) on May 28, 1881, member of the Society of Jesus; created cardinal by John XXIII in 1959.

2   The secretariat presided over by Bea was born as a council secretariat *"ad unitatem Christianorum fovendam."* At first it was charged with all ecumenical action toward non-Catholics and non-Christians. Then it was "redimensioned" and specialized for ecumenical action only toward non-Catholics, while a special secretariat was created for non-Christians under the direction of Cardinal Marella. Monsignor Willebrands is also secretary with Bea.

CHAPTER XIV

1   Franziskus König, born in Rabenstein on August 3, 1905. He was created cardinal by John XXIII, is Archbishop of Vienna, and is president of the Secretariat for Non-Believers.

2   See documents number 201 and 202 of the *Documentatie centrum Concilie.*

3   See Augusto Del Noce, *L'ateismo contemporaneo* (Bologna, 1960).